PRAISE FOR KUNDALINI WONDER

I have just spent days reading, simmering, rereading, dreaming on your most amazing book. I love it. It has helped me so much with the piece I am working on and deepened my awareness, insights, reinforced my own experiences, given me new ways to look at things. . . Kundalini Wonder is one of the clearest, most inspired, humble, authentic, poetic books I have read on the Kundalini experience. How perfect that reading a guide book on awakening becomes an ecstatic experience in itself. May this book lift and inspire the "seed people" so that this new world may be born.

— Eve Ensler, playwright, performer, feminist, activist, *The Vagina Monologues, The World's Body, I Am an Emotional Creature*

While in the crucible of deep soul transformation, where the purifying and revelatory fire of god's grace, known as Kundalini in the yogic tradition, melts away all that limits our consciousness, most people can't give words to the effects of such unspeakable power. Yet, Dorothy Walters manages to express her experiences and reflections even as she continues in the alchemical processes wrought by Shakti Kundalini. Her writings are a chronicle of her soul's work-in-progress that includes revelations, contemplations, and inspired poetry. She offers these not as dogma or perfected wisdom, but as another way of revealing and celebrating how Kundalini graces an individual with myriad gifts through the continuous creative unfolding of Divine Consciousness. You'll want to return often to Dorothy's wellspring bubbling up through *Kundalini Wonder.*

— Lawrence Edwards, Ph.D., author of *Awakening Kundalini: The Path to Radical Freedom, Kali's Bazaar, and The Soul's Journey: Guidance from the Divine Within.* Founder and director of the Anam Cara Meditation Foundation. President of the Kundalini Research Network

The latest book of Dorothy Walters is a considerable offering. She allows that there is "an abundance of material today about awakening" – and there is. But not an abundance of honest, wise guidance about the realities of this transit and the stages of evolution. Her fresh thinking is both challenging, and its own light. She concludes, "We do not leave the world, but become more fully in it…offering service and beauty." You will benefit greatly from her words and her heart.

— Paula D'Arcy, writer and speaker, *Gift of the Red Bird and Stars at Night*

In *Kundalini Wonder* Dorothy Walters offers a tapestry of authentic personal stories, lucid reflections, and ecstatic poems that together weave a magic carpet that can transform us. Now in her ninth decade, she embodies a rapturous, childlike wonderment—clearly the harvest of her spontaneous Kundalini awakening. That's the thing about waking up. Rather than rendering us pompous religious experts, it turns each of us into a holy wild child. I want to be like Dorothy Walters when I grow up. A full-bodied encounter with this book feels like a step in that direction.

— Mirabai Starr, *CARAVAN OF NO DESPAIR: A Memoir of Loss and Transformation; God OF LOVE: A Guide to the Heart of Judaism, Christianity & Islam; WILD MERCY;* translator of John of the Cross and Teresa of Avila

BOOKS BY DOROTHY WALTERS

The Kundalini Poems: Reflections of Radiance and Joy

Unmasking the Rose: A Record of a Kundalini

Initiation (Hampton Roads)

Some Kiss We Want: Poems Selected and New
(Emergent Education Press, second edition)

Marrow of Flame: Poems of the Spiritual Journey

A Cloth of Fine Gold: Poems of the Inner Journey

The Ley Lines of the Soul: Poems of Ecstasy and Ascension

Penelope's Loom: Poems of Turning Matter into Spirit

"Kundalini and the Mystical Journey," lead article in the anthology Kundalini
Rising from Sounds True

Moonlight on a Night Moth's Wing (collages with text by Dorothy Walters and
background art by Rashani Rea)

(All of the above available from Amazon and B&N)

Flannery O'Connor (now out of print)

I Hear My Sisters Saying: Poems of Twentieth Century Women
(co-editor with Carol Konek) (now out of print)

Other sources:

www.kundalinisplendor.blogspot.com
(Poems and Reflections on the Spiritual Journey)

Facebook: Dorothy Walters page

Links to some of Dorothy's online resources can be found at
www.dorothywalters.com

Many poems included in anthologies and elsewhere

Several poems set to music by various composers, sung at Harvard, Royal
Opera House seminar rooms, Boulder Resonance Chorus and elsewhere.

KUNDALINI WONDER

The god/goddess in Your Body

KUNDALINI WONDER

THE GOD/GODDESS IN YOUR BODY

by Dorothy Walters, Ph.D.

KUNDALINI WONDER
THE GOD/GODDESS IN YOUR BODY
by Dorothy Walters

ISBN-13: 978-1-7346284-1-8

Emergence Education Press
P.O. Box 63767, Philadelphia, PA 19147
www.EmergenceEducation.com

Cover photography and design by Silvia Rodrigues

For more information about Dorothy Walters visit:
www.DorothyWalters.com

*This book is dedicated
to all who have experienced the
embrace of the goddess Kundalini
and to all those who seek her sanction.*

ACKNOWLEDGEMENTS

Many thanks to Lawrence Edwards, for allowing me to quote his reflections on Signs and Symptoms of Kundalini awakening.

I also wish to acknowledge the following for the invaluable advice and encouragement they have given to me to make my life as well as this book possible:

Diane Knoll
Claudia Helade
Ann Rick
Hélène des Rosiers
Stephanie Marohn
Karen Lester
Kathy Fowler
Patricia Lay-Dorsey
Peggy Wrenn
Dawn Hartman
Mark Griffith
Gina Barnett
Gail Thompson
Philip Overbaugh
Craig Johnson
Helen Purdum
Jan Elvee
Carol Konek
Susan Walters
Jacqueline and Ed Arnold
Rose Roberts
Susan Decker
Candice and Rob Wagoner
Julie Pogachefsky
Brenda McMorrow
Erica Taxin Bleznak
Valerie A Szarek
Kathe Huntley

…my glory was to have such friends.

—William Butler Yeats

Contents

To the Beloved Who is Shiva

I do not want
to lead someone somewhere.

Nor do I wish to break
some sort of ceiling.

I just wish to be here
with my Beloved,
the one with
the tossing hair,
his body half man,
half woman,
and all in between.

World aflame,
eternal dance.

Everywhere is where He is,
where I would become.

*What is Kundalini? Kundalini is god
moving through your body.*

—UNKNOWN SAGE

INTRODUCTION

Kundalini Awakening is a term often heard in today's world, but many are not aware of its sacred connections and profound implications for the awakening of the soul. Large numbers practice forms of yoga presumably associated with the Kundalini process, but often these are done as little more than physical exercises, executed with little background knowledge of the sacred origins and divine nature of this ancient practice.

At the same time, more and more people are reporting authentic Kundalini Awakenings, these often occurring spontaneously in unexpected settings. Sometimes the cause is a life crisis, physical or psychological, that creates a "space" into which the divine elements may flow. Other times the student's own energies are activated by a guru or special teacher, who offers "shaktipat" (transmission of energies from master to aspirant through deliberate intention).Sometimes the trigger is travel to a sacred location, such as India or Machu Picchu or the Blue Mosque in Turkey, where mystical consciousness is awakened in significant ways.

Indeed, there are many causes and types of awakening.

Some people awaken quickly and unexpectedly. They may open in a moment, in a manner that seems quite foreign to them at the time. The results may be startling. Some may awaken into bliss, others into pain or other disconcerting symptoms, both forms perhaps the precursors of a long and challenging time of adjustment to come. It may then take them years to balance out and learn to deal with the new energies moving within. Whatever the nature of the awakening, it involves a total readjustment of the self, the body, and its consciousness, as a new being is formed.

Others may open in a less dramatic, more gradual fashion. Rather than the fast track, they choose (or are destined to follow) a gentler path, with soft infusions of divine love (or perhaps recurrent discomfort) entering their lives for long periods of time before full awakening occurs. They may follow some specific way of meditating or moving or doing—perhaps they pursue a goal of compassionate service, one of the most valid paths to the state we call "enlightenment."

My own opening was of the first kind and it involved occasional pain as well as acute bliss. Like many who undergo such dramatic experiences, I was in a state of emotional distress at the time. A long-term relationship seemed to be falling apart. For me, the prospect was devastating. It was as if I had fallen into a dark pit, as if the very foundations of my life were crumbling. I knew there was no use in trying to protest or change the situation. I resigned myself to what appeared to be my inexorable fate. I simply gave up and felt myself as nothingness, a being of no consequence. In other words, I experienced ego death.

In this moment of emptiness, Kundalini rushed in. In the blink of an eye, I experienced total transcendence, and knew that whatever I might be, this "Other," this huge dynamic force, was the final reality, and I was merely an infinitesimal speck, a tiny vessel through which it flowed. In other words, I realized that I did not exist except as a creation of my own imagination. Only It, this vast, surging field of energy and love, was real.

This is how it happened: I was sitting in my living room one morning in 1981, full of grief and dismay at the turn my life was taking, and reading a book on comparative mythology. However, this book mentioned Kundalini—how it was an energy that existed at the base of the spine, how it could be lifted into the crown which would then open like a lotus unfolding as proof of enlightenment.

Two illustrations in the book caught my attention. One was a photograph of the famous Bernini statue of St. Teresa of Avila in her encounter with the angel who pierced her heart with his lance, thus opening her to ecstatic divine love. The other was also a representation of rapture, the famous Eastern depiction of the god and goddess (Shiva/Shakti, Yab/Yum) in sexual union. This is an image that has shocked many who do not realize that ecstasy itself is often the indication of divine union, that god is a lover as well as a friend or father/mother.

As I gazed on the Shiva/Shakti image, I tried to awaken my own resting energies of Kundalini. I knew little or nothing about the latter. Indeed, I had never before seriously meditated or done energetic awakening exercises or practiced yoga. I had not even had a massage. The energy body was essentially an unknown to me. I knew virtually nothing of Eastern spiritual writings. I had been a teacher all of my professional life, and now was a professor of English and Women's Studies at a Midwestern state university in Kansas. Of course, I was familiar with the symbology of the archetypal forms. And indeed, I had read widely in such writers as

Jung, Eliade, Blofeld, and Campbell. I had explored the Seth books and the esoteric writings of Yeats and dipped into Madame Blavatsky. I had encountered the Tarot and written poems on the major arcana. I had read Gopi Krishna's account of his own famous awakening experience. I was familiar with the great classics of Western literature: Dante, Milton, Shakespeare, Goethe and others of that rank. I was familiar with the poetry of T. S. Eliot and W. B. Yeats. I had in fact undergone a psychic opening a few years before, but had backed away when the experience became too intense and indeed frightening.

But this morning, I sat on my elm-tree-lined street in Kansas, focusing on my breathing and thinking about ways to raise the Kundalini energies into my head.

Conditions in my life had conspired to produce a dramatic and unforeseen moment that would change my life irrevocably.

In an instant it happened. Swiftly my energies (now highly ecstatic) shot from my base into my head. I fell headlong into the ocean of divine love, my crown opening like a thousand lotus petals, just as the ancient Eastern texts describe. I was swept away in a current of cosmic energy so extreme that I was carried out of myself, into another realm where "I" did not exist, and only this immeasurable dynamic force, this ultimate source of all being and reality, was real. I remained in this state for several minutes, sensuous rapture vibrating in every cell including my head.

I now went into a light trance state that lasted for several days. I held the *vajra* and the bell (sacred implements essential to Tibetan Buddhist initiation). My "vajra" was a small glass barbell-shaped object, my bell a tiny instrument that had once been my mother's. In the course of this initiation, I stood before the mirror and saw the light around my body and heard (inwardly) my new name. Later I learned that I had, intuitively, recreated virtually all the stages of a first-level Buddhist initiation.

Meanwhile, the raptures (for which I had no name) continued with such intensity that I finally gave up and lay down on the carpet and spread out my arms, saying, "Here I am, god, take me."

This pivotal incident shaped the rest of my life. Once the energies are awakened in such intensity, they return again and again, re-configuring and reforming the life in dramatic and unexpected ways. The nervous system undergoes extreme re-patterning. It becomes something other, a receptacle of divine love that never returns to its former state.

The episode I have described took place almost forty years ago, at a time when Kundalini was virtually unknown in the West. Today, there is an abundance of information on this subject, with many books and articles available, both in print and through the internet. Kundalini yoga studios and classes are commonplace and the topic itself is widely known. But I knew no one who had even heard of this phenomenon, and there were no gurus—and indeed very few yoga teachers—where I lived. So I trudged ahead on my own, keeping daily trysts with the Beloved that often produced indescribable bliss, and sometimes bringing a descent into pits of despair or discomfort as the sacred energies opened new pathways within. With no teacher or guide, I followed the direction of the "guru inside," whom I later thought of as the "Beloved Within."

I should here add that although my original experience did involve an ascent of the energies up the spine to the crown, soon they manifested as a diffuse, all over blissful state which ultimately touched and transformed every single molecule and fiber of my body as the subtle body awoke to consciousness.

I told almost no one of my transformation. It was a secret so vast, so filled with awe and wonder that I felt it would be a kind of sacrilege to share it. And when I did attempt (ultimately) to tell my experience to certain "authorities," I got such answers as, "If you are lucky, you will get over this," and "No, the texts do not include anything such as this. The energies may be hot or cold or like electricity, but there is no mention of what you describe." After many years of silence, I met Andrew Harvey in San Francisco in the mid-nineties and he understood the tale I so hesitantly described. He urged me to write about my experiences. At his insistence and with his help, I published my personal account of this transcendent opening and its consequences in a book called, "Unmasking the Rose: A Record of a Kundalini Initiation" (2002), as well as several books of spiritual poetry inspired by this experience. More recently, I published a collection called "Some Kiss We Want: Poems Selected and New," that is a compilation of the best of these poems, written over many years. In 2018, I published "The Kundalini Poems: Reflections of Radiance and Joy," as a kind of culmination of my long journey into divine union.

And Kundalini Wonder (this present volume) will be available soon.

In 2004, I began a blog on Kundalini (www.Kundalinisplendor.blogspot. com), one of the first spiritual blogs to appear on the internet. I currently do a Facebook page on Kundalini and similar subjects. I have posted numerous poems and reflections on this and related topics, with many observations on the nature and meaning of the Kundalini process and its impact on those touched by its transformational energies. Although Kundalini is now much more widely known than it was in that earlier time, there still remains much misunderstanding regarding its essential nature and manifestation. This present book is neither a manual of instruction nor a repetition of information now easily obtainable elsewhere. It is a volume unlike any other, looking at Kundalini from varied perspectives, describing some of the actual experiences that one may undergo during the process of unfolding, and considering what this spreading phenomenon means to humankind as we move together into new states of awareness.

As a result of such public sharing, I now hear often from others undergoing the Kundalini process, and I offer them encouragement and advice as to how to proceed. I do not charge for these responses, since I feel that part of my "assignment" at this stage is to contribute in every way I can to what I feel is a worldwide awakening process, a planetary initiation into new forms of consciousness as human evolution carries us to expanded levels of being. I believe that through the operation of Kundalini, we are indeed becoming the "divine human," the Adam Kadmon of the Kabbalah, the dross turned to gold of the alchemists, those moving toward the Omega Point described by Teilhard de Chardin. We still have far to go, and hence my title refers primarily to the future human, not ourselves as we are in our present state, for we are still involved in the birth struggle of this emergent being. But even now, we are permitted glimpses and tastes of the transfigured self that is to come.

This book invites the practitioner—as well as the interested reader—to pause and reflect on the Kundalini process itself. It contains brief musings and commentary on various aspects of this great Mystery—for no one knows exactly what Kundalini is—its ultimate source is still hidden, but each moment of inner rapture is felt unmistakably as divine union, indeed as if one had been in fact entered by a loving god or goddess, a reality far beyond comprehension yet undeniable in its expression.

This collection does not contain detailed instruction on how to awaken the inner energies, nor does it explain at length the various terms common to Kundalini Yoga, such as chakras, nadis and the like. Such information is now readily available from myriad sources. It is not written from the perspective of a particular lineage or tradition, but rather offers insights garnered over many years by a "solitary practitioner," one who discovered the realities of the journey—the delights as well as the struggles—through many years of sacred and solitary practice.

Much of my experience involved states of bliss or rapture, but it should be kept in mind that although such experiences are indeed somatic and quasi-erotic, they are not explicitly sexual. Rather, they are a form of sublimated energy, spiritual love in its highest manifestation. The Beloved Within is real, not a fancy.

Today, information on the current "shift" is arriving at a breathless pace, from all directions, and from a variety of sources. Most of these share a central truth—indeed this is a truth that needs to be expressed again and again, in many different ways by many voices. It is like the energy of a gathering storm—a storm of extreme transformation, the arrival of a new way of perception, the time of humanity's actual ascent to a higher level of consciousness. It is the critical moment we have waited for so long, and indeed the reason why we came—to be participants, to do our bit to lift the vibrations of ourselves and the world around us in a collective transfiguration.

This transformation is happening in a time of deep crisis. Humanity appears to be facing a threat unlike any we have known before. We are warned that we face the possibility of planet death and the extinction of our species because of changing climate. Forces of terror and greed are being unleashed across the globe, and here in our own country. But, like the flower that emerges from the ash of the volcano, positive change is emerging even in the midst of disaster, movement upward as well as destruction of our present outer structures and notions of reality.

It is imperative that although we acknowledge the shadow, we continue to stand in and embrace the light. Because of my own abrupt transfiguring experience, I believe that "anything can happen to anyone at any time under any circumstances." Who knows what massive shifts will take place, even what interventions may occur?

Whatever it is, we can agree on one thing—"something is happening."

Hence I offer these reflections honoring the divine force that is propelling us forward on this exciting upward movement. Kundalini, when widely experienced, can carry us toward "enlightenment," the new stage of human development, the goal we have sought and treasured for so long. The divine human is becoming a real possibility, and many are discovering its truth.

It is my hope that you will find this book useful in your own sacred journey and that you too will become an advocate and helper in this, our common process of transfiguration.

What is it?

It has to do
with love.

It has to do with energy.

It has to do with the god force energy
that runs through everything.

It has to do with how we feel
when we are finally connected.

It is god
moving through your body.

It is the Beloved making love
with you from within,
even when you are not
expecting it.

It is you
coming home to yourself
at last.

PREFACE

Many of those who write about the shift into a new consciousness, speak as if the change were primarily mental—a new perspective, a different way of seeing things. Such an intellectual shift is indeed paramount, but these perspectives exclude a more fundamental aspect—the transformation of the body itself and its many elements into the new configuration of the future human.

What if the change involved the self in the most radical way? What if the "body" now had totally new capacities—to feel, to experience, to know through the sensate system the entire world and its contents in a novel and totally different mode?

What if lovers (and all would then be lovers of each other) discovered and entered one another in the fashion (I believe) that the angels do—as clouds of feeling fusing and then dispersing as they pass through one another? Gender issues as such would be irrelevant, for there would be no assigned "genders"—all would be beyond male/female and exist as pure being, the way "ultimate essence" (god, angels) is/are now. What if another's pain was felt with the same intensity as one's own? What if compassion were a mark of one's own deeply experienced identification with the wounded one's own pain? Would this not do a great deal to annihilate war, murder, mayhem of all sorts?

What if group souls of those with like essences were formed, in which each participated the ideas and feelings of the others (though still retaining a personal identity)?

Is Kundalini itself—with its charged feelings, its resonance with all creation including not only the physical settings but the emanations from the persons it is transfiguring—a move in this direction? Anyone who has resonated deeply from a passage in music, wept before the beauty of mountain or flower, or thrilled to a lover's touch understands this way of knowing. It involves perception, but is not limited to mental thought processes. It offers a way of participating in/with the universe unlike what is produced by mathematical formula or artificial "intelligence." Robots are not people. They may act on command, but they do not feel.

And feeling itself, incorporated into and reinforcing mental processes, is the basis of the new evolutionary stage.

Are we even now entering this critical stage of transition? Are even the New Age seekers, the followers of sometimes specious gurus, the still "green" would-be wisdom writers who are yet not really qualified to speak—part of an already happening process?

Are we building toward a "tipping point," where the new being will emerge fully clad in its glory?

Those among us who already participate in the new paradigm (though in limited ways), those who open to the bliss of groups vibrating to the same frequency in harmony, those who have tasted rapture as music, as movement, as joy of the word—they are the way showers, the pilgrims who offer their essence in all its aspects and levels, to the shift that is taking place. They often in effect are willing to climb onto the altar as sacrifice in order to share, for they yield much of their familiar identities and personae to be shredded in the service of the emergent being, the "divine human."

Yeats said, "Man can embody truth but never know it." Embodied truth is that which is felt, realized through moments of divine union, an actual somatic, sometimes erotic, plunging into those invisible realms where ultimate reality (the ongoing Mystery) exists.

We cannot know or adequately define god/goddess, but we can feel her in our bodies. We can connect on an undeniable level with that great power/ energy that surges through the cosmos, brings into being all that is, and lifts us into states of blissful connection that are, inevitably, beyond words, yet proof that we ourselves are not defined by the material components that make up our bodies and surroundings, but rather we are infinitesimal particles in the unfathomable forces that comprise the "everything" that is. It is our own subjective experiences that tell us we inhabit a "cosmic love field," invisible and often undetected, yet is the ultimate reality that can be experienced once we are in proper alignment.

Thus, this is a book about, and some reflections on, feeling itself—in particular, the inner sensations of delight and joy (as well as the challenges) that arise through the awakening of the Kundalini energies within the "self" and the implications of this transformation.

The ancient ones knew that it is through Kundalini that the energies are aroused and then ascend to join the very crown in ecstatic delight. For the crown then opens, like a thousand petaled lotus, to receive the infusions of divine love that come pouring in, and thus join human and the invisible Other in holy union.

This state is that which the alchemists of all ages have sought to achieve: the transformation of dull matter into the gold of the transfigured human.

It is Shiva/Shakti in ecstatic union. It is Adam Kadmon of the Kabbalah. It is the light body of contemporary literature, the Merkabah rider's goal of springing to heaven as described in earlier eras. It is Teilhard's Omega point, where god and human merge. It is the Shaman's voyage to the world beyond time.

It is what Shri Aurobindo foretold in his visionary writings. It is what Gopi Krishna predicted in his prophetic works.

It is a taste of Enlightenment itself, the state that many have yearned for and sacrificed much to attain.

Though such transcendent moments are sometimes temporary, they offer us glimpses of a condition beyond the mundane, and reveal realms that exist beyond the human ordinary. These are the times of arrival, the coming home, the knowing of who you really are.

This book is the result of an ongoing effort to explore and experience the essence of this inner journey, to describe as far as possible, the feeling level of transcendent experience, and thus to validate what it is possible to "know," not only by weights and measures but by immersion into the Love Field which surrounds us and is our authentic home. It describes a journey of over thirty years. I offer these thoughts in the hope that they will aid and assist all now participating (in whatever way) in this universal phenomenon of supreme transformation.

part 1

AWAKENING TO ECSTASY

A THOUSAND YEARS

Dancer among dancers,
I danced my way
to the moment
which cannot be told.

O, such astonishment
and joy. . .
fulfillment at last . . .

Mind possessed,
soul set wild to sing
its own sacred hymns
of holy desire
in that instant which lasted
a thousand years.

NOT IN KANSAS ANYMORE

In 1981, I was 53 years old. It was Kansas and it was hot, in the way that only Kansas can be in the summer. It was the kind of temperature where people say you can cook an egg on the pavement. I was a professor at a state university where I was teaching women's literature and directing our women's studies program, which I and my colleagues had launched a few years before. People often look surprised when I tell them that ours was one of the earlier programs in the country, but I then respond that, "Yes, and the women of Kansas were really ready for us."

I had for some time been interested in certain esoteric subjects. I had studied the Kabbalah and the mystic paths of the Tarot deck. I had explored various systems of spiritual transformation (how to change the base metal of human nature into gold, as the earlier alchemists described it.) Jung's work on alchemical transformation had been extremely valuable here, and also Mircea Eliade's books on Shamanism, where I learned that the fusion of opposites was essential to all initiations. I had read the Seth material and experimented a bit with telepathic communication, sometimes with startling results.

I had also dabbled with Ouija work and watched in amazement as the board and our hands took on an eerie glow as the planchette skipped across the board. We received fascinating messages from a spirit who identified himself as "MKBL," a designation we took for "Master of the Kabbalah." This communicator was quite formal in his answers, even using the perfect tense (as in "If I were" instead of "If I was.")

Because I had obtained a Ph.D. in English and American literature, I was familiar with much of the wisdom contained in the Western classics. Indeed, my teachers were Dante, Shakespeare, Milton, Thoreau, and such. I had gained much insight through these readings. (It was only later that I, like many others, discovered the contributions of women writers, then and now. In those days, female writers were barely alluded to, if at all.)

But more important that any of these teachers was my discovery of the Great Mother. I found her in the early seventies through Eric

Neuman's groundbreaking book called simply, The Great Mother. The Mother goddess is a powerful archetype and she now fully occupied my consciousness. I wrote poems to her and gave talks to our various classes about her identity and nature. To my delight, these Kansas women were fascinated to learn that there had been a time, in Merlin Stone's words, "When god was a Woman." I traveled in Greece and sensed the goddess' presence everywhere, especially around Delphi and Eleusis, and had a deep sense of connection with the land itself, perhaps from some earlier life there with the women's cults. Thoughts of the High Priestess, the Oracle at Delphi—these sounded strong chords within.

Through teaching women's studies, I understood more fully the connection between male and female balance within each of us. I thought about the difference between patriarchal and matriarchal societies and approaches, the difference between intuition and logic, the receptive vs. the controlling, yin and yang.

But none of these had prepared me for what was to take place now. This strange and unplanned event was to change my life forever, and carry me into a world I had not dreamed existed. The event would unfold as a series of constant swings between ecstasy and discomfort, rapture and grief, as new elements and unknown frequencies entered my body and sought to attain balance within.

What happened to me is known as Spontaneous Kundalini Awakening.

Here is how it occurred.

THE CONTEXT

I had been in a long-term relationship that had seemed near perfection. We were wonderfully matched on all levels—mental, emotional, sexual. We shared an intimacy that is rare in relationships. We had, in fact, essentially "merged."

Often we did not need to speak our thoughts aloud, for each inwardly sensed what the other was thinking. Even in sleep, we sometimes conversed, as she spoke in her sleep and I answered her either aloud or—at times—by simply silently thinking my replies. She revealed the contents of her unconscious in a way that would have delighted Freud. Often she spoke in the voice of a child, and even composed little poems befitting a very young poet. Sometimes it was as though spirits drifting through her psyche spoke through her, in various guises that suggested who they were. ("I rang the bell for you, Isho, and I wept for you. I wept.")

We had together explored many paranormal phenomena, with occasional impressive results. Thus, when we dabbled with telepathic communication using our new and unfamiliar Tarot deck as our focus, she (as receiver) was able to describe the images on the first four cards I drew with great precision. But when I drew the fifth card, I realized it was a repetition of one we had already used and put it back into the deck, whereupon she announced, "We've had this one before."

Another incident: We were playing a card game in which the two players each lay out a line of 10 or 12 cards along the (opposite vertical) sides of the board (using separate decks). The idea, as I recall, was to get rid of your remaining cards, by playing them on either your own or your opponent's cards. This day, when we each lined up our rows, we saw that our lineups were in fact mirror images of each other (though in reverse order), as if some unseen hand had intervened, playing a kind of prank on our startled selves.

We had together dabbled in Ouija work, and watched in fascination as our hands and the board itself lit up with a kind of eerie green gold light, and the planchette flew from one letter to the next.
However, in the spring of 1981, everything changed and this idyllic

relationship came to an end. My partner (whom I will call Kate for this telling) developed an infatuation with one of her male professors and told me she wished to have a relationship with him. I appreciated her honesty, and I was devastated. I had experienced several earlier heartbreaks (similar in kind) and had, perhaps against my better judgment, entered into this connection with certain misgivings. Still, I had held nothing back, for our experience seemed like something foreordained, even karmic in nature.

I did not protest her intentions. I simply gave up, stepped aside, and agreed to let her follow her longings. I felt as though the earth had given way under my feet, that I was once again in my life accounted as nothing, a non-being who had no right even to be considered. In other words, I experienced deep ego death.

It was during this state, when a "space" was created in my psyche, that the event occurred which was, in Katherine Anne Porter's words (in another context) "the moment that changed everything."

Although I did not realize it, this was the moment I had been preparing for all of my life.

Many people think sex when they hear the word Kundalini. They are drawn to pursue awakening because they are hoping to have more intense and pleasurable sexual experiences.

And, indeed, they are partially right. Many people find they are suddenly more "turned on," readier to pursue new sexual adventures, and possibly experience new levels of excitement and gratification, once Kundalini becomes active in consciousness.

Indeed, an old saying is that someone who is undergoing Kundalini awakening is "irresistible." This may or may not be true, but the truth is that someone in the early stages of awakening may "emanate" an energy that draws others into their orbit like a magnet. And some, such as certain gurus and spiritual teachers, may continue to send out such signals as their bodies radiate "divine energies" into the environment. Sometimes students are so drawn to these "frequencies" that they will literally follow the guru around to experience these exquisite vibrations. I have been told by those in the inner circle of one famous guru that young women sought to sit near him in satsang in order to experience his "vibes"—and in fact that some experienced orgasms as a result.

I have known spiritual teachers whose energy field was so intense that I went into "bliss" states (but certainly not orgasm) just by entering the room where they were present. I have had friends whose spiritual bodies were so purified that they too emanated sweet energies that one could detect and resonate with just by being near them. One woman's early stage Kundalini vibrations were so intense that just placing my hand near her back was enough to awaken strong ecstatic (and erotic) resonance in my own system.

So, let's be clear. Kundalini energy is closely akin to sexual energy, and yet, there is a difference. Kundalini is not sexual energy per se, but it can definitely carry an erotic tone. As one woman noted, "I get it. Kundalini is like sex only different."

What, then, is the difference? From my own experience, I have drawn some tentative conclusions, so what follows is merely speculation on my part.

First, Kundalini bliss or ecstasy does not necessarily arise from a specifically sexual trigger (though even here, one has to pause and remember that in ancient India sexual arousal was definitely used by males to awaken the energies, which were—in theory—then lifted up the spine to the head. These were prescribed Tantric practices, in which the female was used, for the most part, merely to stimulate the erotic desire of the male—the texts describe only the male experience, for apparently women were not eligible to become Kundalini initiates through this method.)

For me, in fact, my original experience of awakening (now nearly 50 years ago) did occur, oddly enough, from a similar pattern, not by design but by accident. I had unintentionally recreated (with my partner) this ancient Tantric practice—arousal without release.

It was as if a scenario had been prepared and now was being enacted. A short time later when I was alone, I read from a book that mentioned Kundalini, but said nothing about how to awaken it. On impulse, I decided I too could bring these wondrous energies from the base to the crown, a feat that under normal circumstances should have been impossible. I meditated on the god and goddess (Shiva/Shakti) in union (another Tantric practice, but one quite foreign to me) and this became the trigger for the awakening itself, when rapturous energies shot from the lower chakras straight into my head and into my opening crown. I had been immersed in the new field of women's studies and as a result had studied both male and female energies. Now I had "thrown myself" (mentally and energetically) into the female form, then into the male image and finally into the two embracing.

Thus "sexual" energies came into play in this initial awakening, but they were quickly transmuted into spiritual energies. I never repeated this original experience, for once the energies are aroused, they often continue to manifest as bliss/ecstasy, as if the body automatically transforms what was before sexual into the undeniable spiritual.

The energies I experienced then, and for the many years that followed, were indeed not sexual, but sex transmuted into what was itself acutely ecstatic, bliss carried to the extreme throughout the body, a fully charged rapturous experience, as delight flowed into all the parts of the body, in ever more subtle ways. Each moment of such experience felt totally sacred, as if one were mating with a god, merging with the divine in holy union. These times of blessed fusion never involved any kind of touching, but were triggered by simple stimuli, such as reading a sacred poem, listening to sacred music, or performing extremely subtle moves (such as moving the arm up and down, sometimes merely flexing the fingers in imperceptible ways).

Thus my body (the nervous system) was in effect remade, becoming ever more sensitive to all stimuli, both good and bad, and opening to ever more subtle effects.

WHAT IS KUNDALINI?

Of all human phenomena, Kundalini is one of the most mysterious and least understood. According to ancient yogic texts, Kundalini is a serpent resting at the base of the spine. When aroused, it ascends in spiral fashion through the various chakras (wheels) of the body until it reaches the crown, where its energies unite with those of the immensity which sustains all. At that moment, the small self loses itself in forgetfulness, and regains its primal condition as part of the ever-flowing consciousness which is the final reality. This—a state of unimaginable bliss—is known as enlightenment.

Kundalini means "coiled," for in Hindu symbology the snake is coiled two and a half times in its resting place. Each chakra is an energy center, a "wheel" which presumably begins to spin as the energy passes through. On each side of the spinal column is a major channel for ascent, one known as Ida and the other Pingala. These form a helix around the central channel, the Sushumna, a tiny thread rising from the base to the very top of the spinal column.

Many devout students of yoga devote their lives to perfecting the technique of awakening and then lifting the Kundalini energies. To this end, they adhere to a strict yogic discipline, including the practice of asanas (positions), a restricted diet, and performance of austere purification rituals. Only the very pure in body and spirit are deemed fit to follow this path with impunity. Those less prepared expose themselves to dangers of every sort, from physical illness to emotional unbalance. Because of the difficulties inherent in the practice, the student is cautioned to proceed only under the guidance of an experienced teacher. Once the technique is mastered, the student is said to be gifted with many "supernatural" powers—such as the ability to see or hear at a distance, to travel out of body, and to charm without effort.

Kundalini has also played a prominent role in many other cultures, where it has been a key element in spiritual practice. Kundalini (under various names) has been identified as central to such spiritual traditions as the esoteric practices of early Egypt, Taoism and yoga in Asia, and shamanism throughout the world. Some feel that even the ecstatic states reported in mystic Christianity reflect the workings of Kundalini. Kundalini, by whatever name, is universally treasured as a sacred experience, and venerated as a means of passage to other worldly realms.

In contemporary thought, Kundalini is widely viewed as the essential electromagnetic psycho/spiritual system which undergirds and sustains all of the operations of the self—from physical to mental to emotional. This guiding force generally operates below the level of consciousness, keeping the body in balance and performing in a "normal" fashion. However, spontaneous Kundalini experiences—even full awakening— can occur. Unexpected arousal is being reported more and more frequently across the globe. In the majority of cases, this "awakening" is imbued with a deeply spiritual cast. It generally begets in the subject a response of humility and awe. The seeker is now able to experience states far transcending anything known before. It is as if she now thinks and feels at the "cellular" level, with a capacity for knowing deeper and swifter than any perception achieved through the familiar "rational" mind. She may now be vulnerable to states of both ecstasy and pain beyond any previously imagined. Some may develop rare healing powers or acute mental abilities. In its perfect manifestation, Kundalini purges the self of all its latent illness and psychological perturbation, leaving a being empowered to express her fullest potential.

Gopi Krishna maintained that Kundalini would be the engine for the evolutionary transformation of humanity. Those who experience its high bliss and overwhelming sense of connectedness to divine purpose and direction concur. Whatever else it does, Kundalini permanently changes the nervous system, making it capable of states of awareness well beyond the familiar spectrum. These changes lead to a shift not merely in what we see but how we see. The threshold is lowered for both pleasure and pain, the defenses are stripped away. One experiences the inter-connectedness of all beings and levels in the most personal and intimate sense—one resonates at the deepest centers with this new found knowledge.

Kundalini opens the system to infusions of the divine; one is held by unmitigated, unimaginable, pure love. And this love is the sustaining force of the cosmos itself.

(from *Unmasking the Rose, a spiritual memoir*)

In the many years that followed the key moment, the bliss energies continued to visit, sometimes daily, sometimes less frequently, but they gradually became softer and more subtle—the image that comes to mind is of a bonfire that becomes less and less intense over time and then finally exists as a small flame, diminished but still beautiful. For me, the outer lover entered less into awareness until, ultimately, it was the inner Beloved who came through in my practice each morning—when indeed it felt as though some unseen presence was making love to me from within.

But the question I continue to ponder was and *is*, indeed, what is the ultimate difference between such "spiritual energies" and the more familiar sexual energies?

In fact, both rely on the body's natural physio/chemical/biological/ electric/magnetic/psychic system—whatever that may be. The energies come from the same source, but one (the sexual energy) is in fact "transmuted" into the other, which then finds a very different expression. (To transmute simply means to change from one state to another, as, for example, when heated water is transmuted to steam.)

Here are some of the distinctions that I make, but these will not be true for everyone:

Spiritual energy, unlike sexual energy, typically has no sexual trigger, no tactile component, and no specific goal (such as orgasm). The "trigger" could be anything from an inner image to a piece of music to movement to a state of altered consciousness. Something simply starts the flow of inner bliss—and there it is—a meditation of joy, the goddess dancing inside the self.

The feeling tone of this experience is delightful but quite different from sex per se, as mysterious energies move though the physical and subtle systems of the body—the very cells and tissues seem to awaken and celebrate within.

The experience offers a deep sense of connection with the divine—one feels as though one is participating in a sacred ceremony of oneness with the Lover within and that the Lover is of divine origin—indeed it is as if "god is moving through your body." And this is the "goal": to become ever more aligned with that holy source, to allow the inner guide to direct the process, and to know, finally, who we truly are.

The energies can manifest as a kind of reaction to and resonance with certain sacred places on earth (such as "holy Ireland," land of mystic wells and sacred earth centers); certain charged "artifacts" (various artworks, crafted under special conditions by intent artists—such as an ancient Chinese vase fired in the Emperor's kiln, that still carries the vibrations of the original makers; more recent artworks, such as the paintings of Rothko or some of the earlier female impressionists; certain literary texts, such as the poetry of Rumi or Kabir or Hafiz or Mirabai or ancient works such as the *Shaivite Sutras*; or more contemporary writings such as Normandi Ellis' *Awakening Osiris; mantras;* chanting; gentle movement; dancing; and a host of other stimuli, which can trigger Kundalini in a myriad ways.

Certain kinds of music can awaken the inner bliss (I think of Krishna Das, and Brahms' German Requiem—indeed almost any requiem can take us there as well as many other kinds of music, depending on your taste); certain paintings; special people, simply by their presence.

The bliss may flow in areas quite distanced from the sexual centers—it may become an ecstatic rapture in the hands or face or chest—the heart may open in near unbearable joy. It may "turn on" one's feet or elbows or the chakras of the throat or solar plexus or face or crown. It is as if the inner beloved wishes to "touch" and awaken every portion, every cell, every unknown filament and fiber of your body.

I hasten to add that such is not the inevitable progression of Kundalini. For every moment of ecstasy, there may be an equivalent sensation of pain, each infusion of divine bliss may be followed by counterbalancing states of discomfort. The body is challenged to integrate and balance new and higher frequencies into the system and this process may take a long time. Each block, each place of lurking unresolved issues of the psyche and flesh will announce itself unmistakably as pain until the problem area is cleared.

Like a human lover, Kundalini can be tricky and unpredictable. But, unlike the human, it does not leave—for it is the ultimate expression of you yourself, the authentic you. It has been abiding there, waiting in your subconscious all this time (like a serpent at the base of your spine) and now "it," the source, the reality of who you truly are, rises into conscious awareness and you know it as ultimate connection with what we call the "divine" (god with many names). You now realize that you are an infinitesimal particle in this vast ocean of being, and in fact do not exist as a separate identity. This realization is called "Enlightenment." (And some are very angry when they discover their reduced state.) You will not remain in such an exalted condition forever, but you have had a taste, a glimpse of what "enlightenment" consists of. Your job now is to return to the mundane, familiar world, and to learn to exist in it carrying your new knowledge. Indeed, you must now learn to "walk in the two worlds," a task that is not always easy to bear. You are now ready to undergo profound transformation, as every molecule and cell of your body is being transformed into a new configuration, through the alchemy of turning the base metal of the human into the gold of divine being. You are, in fact, being "reborn" in the most profound way possible, and birth is not a painless process.

INTERLUDE: AN UNEXPECTED MOMENT
(A FEW YEARS LATER)

This morning I went into my living room to look for any stray cups or saucers that needed to go into my dishwasher. I had taken only a few steps when I realized my energies were running in a pleasant way through my body. I have not done my "practice" for quite some time—I have had errands to run, walks to take, and poems to write. Somehow I can never seem to get it all in—and thus I sometimes skip my practice (my form of meditation) in favor of other priorities.

But there it came—catching me unawares. So I stopped short, began to move my hands and arms and felt sweet thrills of delight moving here and there, up and down as I moved my hands in circles near my body, palms facing inward, hands about six inches away.

Often one feels the energies more intensely in areas recently exercised and thus "more awake." Lately, I have been walking quite a bit and sure enough, the bliss was especially noticeable in the hip and flank area.

I circled my hands all the way up, then down again, then did shoulder and arm rotation, feet planted firmly but hips moving in a circle along with my moving arms. Everything good. Delicious, in fact.

So—I ask you—is this sex or something other? I think the latter. I call it living room bliss, connection with the divine, god/goddess or at least god's emissary flowing through your body once more. It never ceases!

Listen. . . listen. . .
Can you hear those honeydrops fall
from the mouth of god?
Can you feel the rose
opening in your spine?
Whatever you were before
now you are only this.

****

Does anyone else
feel this love?
Like the breath
of a thousand rose gardens
dreaming they are petals
crushed in god's hand

(from *Some Kiss We Want: Poems Selected and New*)

THE MOST SECRET EXPERIENCE

Of all experiences of the inner self, Kundalini is the most secret, the most protected. It is the most intimate, the most personal. One often does not wish to speak of it because to do so is—as it were—to reveal sacred knowledge, to expose secrets divulged in private to the chosen listener. Kundalini brings us in direct confrontation with that which we are—our quintessential, fundamental self—that range of sensation and patterned feeling, the memory of which we long ago buried in the depths below consciousness, but which may surface, briefly and in disguise, in moments of intense feeling.

But once re-encountered, we know it (the tonos, the way of being) immediately as our very selves, the stranger we have yearned to meet, the god we have sought to know. It confirms the familiar assertion, so often challenged or denied—we and the god are one.

To describe the sensation of Kundalini is like delineating the course of sexual arousal. Can one adequately convey to another—in language — that which is experienced in the realm of pure sensation? I think not. It is personal, unique, part of the individual repertoire of response. By listening to my account of my experience, you may, possibly, relate it to something in your own sphere and judge it to be similar or not. But you can never know the true quality of my subjective response unless you become me, or, like a spirit, enter my system in order to taste with my mouth, sense with my nerves.

ENTERING THE NEXT LEVEL

We are, of course, moving forward, encountering new experiences in our own journeys of transformation all the time. We never stand still, but keep moving on to new stages, unfamiliar and exciting levels of awakening.

But at times, many of us sense a sudden shift into a radically transfigured level of awareness and response, a kind of "quantum leap" into a still more advanced state of our common evolution.

And such swift shifts can be challenging. They may take us into more intense infusions of bliss, or they can awaken old unresolved issues, wounds of body and spirit. If we move ahead too fast, we risk being overwhelmed. If we close to the new energies and the expanded awareness they bring, then we fail to accept our role in this key process and thus fail to realize our life purpose.

Here are some suggestions that I offer as a kind of loose guide for those immersed in this transformative journey:

Be open to what is unfamiliar, but don't lose all your boundaries. Don't be swept away as by a swift current, but don't dam up your inner responses so that your process becomes static and hence begins to wither and die.

Do whatever you need to maintain balance on all levels—whether it is counseling or medical advice, more physical exercise, a change of diet—all these are important. Your body is your physical vehicle and your emotional and mental bodies all have a role to play.

Explore new territory but don't throw away all your maps. Test every "truth" from every source in the fire of your own discriminating mind. Follow Buddha's advice, "Believe nothing just because I have said it. Weigh it in the scales of your own rational mind."

Examine diverse views, various perspectives, even those that seem too "weird" or "far out" to be credible. Often there is a kernel of truth even in the most seemingly outrageous perspectives. Extract what is valuable to you, and leave the rest for others.

THE NEW AGE AND ANCIENT TEACHINGS

The New Age has gained a bad name. What began as an attempt to rediscover and revivify ancient wisdom has become diluted, revised, commercialized, and packaged for sale on the marketplace. Yoga, one of the most sacred and indeed esoteric practices for centuries, has, in many venues, become an athletic exercise, devoted to enhancing one's physical strength and appearance. Do yoga to look good is often the theme. Perform asanas so you can sweat and feel better is another.

Now, there is nothing wrong with doing physical exercise to improve one's health and bodily strength. But this is not the purpose of true yoga. The word yoga means (in one interpretation) "yoke." What is yoked is the inner self with the divine source. Each asana, each move, even the flicker of a finger or the turn of an eye, is part of that process of divine union, and blessed is the practitioner who is conscious of this. The enhanced physique, the improved appearance—these may occur as the byproduct, but they are not the purpose of yoga.

The great gods and goddesses whose power was acknowledged and reverenced in the past often become shrunken symbols, worn as ornaments by those who often don't even know their names. The ancient texts are often ignored or diluted so that the core messages are skewed, as if a nourishing soup had literally been watered down for a palate too weak to swallow the pure essence. Modern "prophets" who repackage ancient ideas in forms "suitable for the Western audience" go on TV and make fortunes for their offerings.

I think such activities are diversions, traps to lead us away from the true path. Some, observing the shallowness of much of the contemporary New Age scene, turn away from spiritual pursuits entirely.

But I believe that none of this detracts from the inherent truth and authenticity of the central message, given to us by sages from many eras and societies, and often spoken to us by the "teacher within." The message is simple: we and the Divine Source are one, and the link between us and all other beings in our universe is Love Itself. There is indeed a "jewel in the lotus" but it is up to us to find it.

WHY I BELIEVE IN THE LIGHT BODY

The notion of the light body is not new. It has been referred to in virtually all of the esoteric traditions past and present. Sometimes it is called by another name—the process of creating it may be described as the divinization of matter, creating the Merkabah vehicle, the evolution of consciousness, entering Nirvana, or attaining enlightenment. The Egyptian, Taoist, tantric, and Jewish traditions all have names for a similar or same process.

I believe in this phenomenon because I experience it frequently in my living room when I do my energy practice and feel the energetic shifts occurring, always at a new level. I watch the process unfold as successive layers are peeled away, "like an onion," as some say. I note the increased awareness not only to the inner energy but also to outer things. I sense a transition to an ever higher vibration, as if I am being molded into a "new" being, with a transformed nervous system that more and more feels like it belongs to a being from some other place, so that I am reminded over and over that I am not truly "of this place, of this time," but am an alien among my own species.

And—of course—there are countless others undergoing the same process. When we are lucky enough to find one another, we confide the details of our journey, realizations that the "ordinary, normal" person could not fathom. For the most part, we keep our altered identity secret from others unless we sense that they are like-minded souls.

One friend remarked, "Why should I read scientific books about cellular transformation, when I experience it constantly in my own body?" Indeed, if you are part of the process, you will know it. It is the actual transformation of consciousness (we become aware of an infinitely wider field of possibilities, of ways of experiencing ourselves and the world, than we were aware of before): it is the true evolutionary shift of the species. The notion of a "light body" is not a metaphor, but a reality.

Evolution is not an easy process. We often feel we "signed up" for this mission before we got here. And we sometimes joke among ourselves that we might not have agreed so readily, had we known how difficult and prolonged the journey would be.

But we are here, we are doing it, and more and more of us are involved as we move toward critical mass.

We enter by many portals—Tantric Buddhism, esoteric yoga, esoteric astrology, Taoism, the great mystery religions of Egypt and the Middle East, Sufism, mystical Christianity, mystical Judaism, native shamanism—and many, many others.

All of these are leading us to a similar goal—personal transformation leading to universal initiation.

Kundalini is the driving force behind all of these movements. We feel blessed to be part of the process, for we know this is why we have come.

I gave You
my life, my mind,
my place in the world.

Now I am wondering
what else I might have
to give.

Meanwhile You sit there
smiling.
I am trying to smile
back,
in the midst of this
silence,
the only thing

DANCING WITH BUDDHA

I have left. At the still point of the turning world...
there the dance is...
Except for the point, the still point,
There would be no dance, and there is only the dance.
(T.S. Eliot)

This morning was special. After several days of "no practice," I stood in front of my Buddha thangka and waited (eyes closed), and immediately what flashed into my mind was an image of Buddha, and I was who he was. I sensed the tight curls around my head, the totally composed presence, the quiet contemplation of all that is. And then, I danced.

Now, when I say "dance," I do not mean ordinary rhythmic movements around the room. I stood quite still and moved my arms and hands slightly, gradually shifting into somewhat more clearly defined positions and gestures (body mudras.) What I did was enough. I felt the light move through my body, knew the places that were ready to receive bliss, as well as those in slight distress.

The Buddha within remained still and watching, as the dance took place. Buddha was thus the still point of the turning world, and the dance that occurred was the movement and activity of the stars and the entire universe.

We are, of course, all Buddhas. Buddha in this sense is our Source and our Destination. We have come here to exemplify and express our "Buddha nature" to the fullest.

But—much of the time we forget our essential nature. We go about pursuing the mundane activities of the world, not providing time to remember our irrevocable connection with what is most important of all. Some even squander their energies in actions that harm, rather than help, our world.

Do not forget your Buddha nature (which you of course may name any way you please.) It is there always, waiting for you, for it is you. At times you will contact it and think, oh, yes, this is what I have been seeking for so long. When those times happen, enjoy them fully. They are the inexhaustible fountain of joy, when we become whole and know our true identity.

MAYBE SOMEWHERE

Maybe somewhere there is a monk
chanting
even though he lived
many years before
our time
began.

He is still there
saying his mantra,
Padmasambhava listening,
sacred syllables
reverberating
his flesh.

Sound ascending,
nada brahma.
Hands turning.
Face of light.

This morning, as I listened to a CD of a lama chanting, this poem appeared. And, as the chant continued, I lifted my arms and felt the sweet energies of my aura around my face. As I moved my hands outward, I continued to feel the gentle bliss flows around and over my head. And as I opened my arms even more (now some ten or so inches from my temples), the energies became more and more exquisite. And then I saw (inwardly), first, a goddess with many arms who thus revealed herself in divine currents of feeling, and then, suddenly, a quick vision of the god and goddess in union (the image that began it all for me so many years ago, Shiva and Shakti, male and female, potential and realization, emptiness and the forms of all creation).

Such blessings are bestowed when we offer ourselves to transcendent experience, allowing our vibrations to move to ever higher levels.

ON ECSTASY

Recently, Link TV broadcast a fascinating discussion by Andrew Harvey (Indian born spiritual writer and teacher) and Sobonfu Somé (African born ritualist and healer), on the topic of ecstasy, a state of consciousness that frequently occurs in Kundalini experiences. Many cultures over the world—from early times to the present—include ecstatic states as a feature of their society.

Three primary types of ecstasy were discussed on the program. The first type is when the participant literally "stands outside" him or herself, often losing all awareness of the surroundings, perhaps needing assistance to keep from falling or hurting him/herself or others. This kind of ecstasy is found in tribal cultures, shamanic trance states, oracles of certain lineages. It is wild, unbounded, and, frankly, a bit frightening to observe, since the ecstatic is in a truly ungrounded state and may act in unpredictable ways. Yet such experience has been part of ritual and ceremony from the earliest times.

The second kind of ecstasy is that produced through, for example, techno-rave all-night dances popular in our time, in which the group together gets extremely "high" on the hypnotic beat of the music, the flashing lights of the dance floor, and (for some) drug induced trance states. The collective begins to "vibrate" as one, and all are lifted into some non-ordinary and seemingly pleasurable state.

Another form of ecstatic consciousness is produced by the continuous repetition of sound, as in the practice of Sufi Zikr, where the participants together chant the name of god, moving forward and back in a circle. Sufism itself welcomes ecstatic or trance states, as witnessed in the whirling dances of the sheiks and followers of the Sufi way. Rumi himself apparently partook of trance states, and it was he who practiced and moved forward the Mevlevi order of the "whirling dervishes."

All of these states are rather intense and involve ritualistic forms of awakening the energies within.

Indeed, ecstasy exists in a myriad of forms, with a full spectrum of stages and expressions. In addition to the extreme states of the shamans and rave dancers, there are also softer, more tender, more "delicate" types of ecstatic experience. One need not lose awareness of surroundings, or be stimulated to the verge of possession to know ecstasy. I think Kundalini offers this kind of experience for those whose energies have settled, taken on a more subtle quality. In this state, the energies may feel like light playing over the body—it may feel like one is being stroked by a feather rather than being sounded by a bass drum.

And, amazing as it may seem, these quieter visitations are not necessarily less blissful, less sweet than the more intense forms. Sometimes they can come from actions as simple as stroking the aura, or rolling the eyeballs. As one moves through the Kundalini process, the overall quality of the energies shifts into a kind of "lower gear," where less stimulation is needed to produce (still) fascinating results. Ecstasy may be aroused by simply listening to a piece of sacred music, contemplating a representation of Buddha, reading a sacred poem, gently moving, or even from reading about sacred topics on the computer. Often ecstasy comes as a surprise, an experience familiar but unexpected.

In part, I think these differences of degree and intensity are accounted for by cultural background and individual makeup. Younger and/or more robust participants crave more exciting states. Older and more settled practitioners may need only a subtle cue to enter wondrous bliss states.

In any event, all agree that humans yearn for ecstatic states as a way of escaping the realm of the familiar and ordinary, and entering transcendence.

For many of us, bliss is itself a pathway to the divine essence experienced as the Beloved Within.

A PERFECT DAY

Years ago Eleanor Roosevelt wrote a magazine column called "My Day."
So here is mine:

I knew almost as soon as I got up that this would be one of the "special"
days, when you don't have to look for the inner energies, because they
will find you. So I did my simple "practice" (standing and circling my
body with my hands held a few inches away). And sure enough, here they
came, soft and gentle, like liquid light, here and there, everywhere, with
especial sensation in the face and head, plus hands, arms, and elsewhere.
As always, I am mesmerized, feel like I am getting a "transmission" from
somewhere, wonder if it is a new moon, why the energies are active now.
It started while I was still in the kitchen, and continued even when I
moved to the living room. "Ahhh," I said. "Lovely," I whispered to myself.
"How nice to still be doing this, after so many days of doing other
things, of not doing my practice, of, in fact, being ill perhaps because I
"overdosed" on some of my herbs."

It was as if my "inner guide" had waited for the right moment, and no
outer stimulus was needed.

It has rained with snow mixed in for the last two or three days—no going
for walks, no trees bursting with light—in fact, many of the blooms had
fallen or dulled, as if, well, you had your one day of glory, now spring is
gone and you missed most of it. But, as I started off for my "computer
lesson" on my new Mac (Apple provides wonderful instruction for a year
if you pay an extra $100 and I did), I decided not to bewail my state, but
to feel gratitude for what was given.

And now the snow was melted, day was beautiful, and everything,
especially the lawns and the leaves on the trees had that brand new yellow
green look that comes with the early days of spring. I had a wonderful
lesson, learned many new things (feeling as though I have joined the
cognoscenti, the inner circle of the computer world—not true, but I do
feel empowered to make even this progress), ate at one of my favorite
cafes —and—surrounding the restaurant were the most beautiful

blooming trees (magenta in color) I have ever seen. I had no camera so couldn't photograph them, and I don't know what they were. But they were the splendor of the moment, celebration beyond celebration of the arriving season. So, I felt deep gratitude, for it was indeed a "perfect" day.

KUNDALINI: UNIQUE AND UNIVERSAL

Kundalini is at once the most personal and most universal experience one can have. It strikes at the very heart of the self, touches and transforms it in every imaginable way, and leaves it in a state of unending change and adjustment. Each person undergoes the initiation process in a unique way. The beginning circumstances, the unfolding, the mental and psychological responses are decidedly one's own, unlike anyone else.

Often the initiate's experience is framed in terms already familiar to her: Taoist alchemy, tantric yoga, native American spirituality, goddess lore—whatever has captured her imagination in the past now becomes the template for this overwhelming life event. And the discoveries which manifest during this critical juncture (whether mental or emotional) come as radically new insights, sacred mysteries revealed for the first time.

These revelations are precious, for they carry the initiate into the heart of the sacred, a world one has longed for but never before clearly discerned. The initiation is a gift to be treasured and revered.

At the same time, deep spiritual transformation is a universal human experience, one with a very long history across time and space. Whether it is the journey of the Christian mystic into divine union or the Sufi seeker yearning for the Beloved, the story of the soul's encounter with the inner reality carries certain features common to virtually all traditions and lineages. The classic account of these stages or states is found in Evelyn Underhill's Mysticism, an indispensable guide for all engaged in the spiritual quest.

In addition to the traditional stages of the mystic path discussed by Underhill, there are also certain recurrent motifs or themes that seem to run through many personal accounts. Here are some that come readily to mind:

(Actually, some of these may overlap with Underhill's broader categories—here I am simply reviewing certain features of my own experience that are echoed or mirrored in the descriptions of others, past and present.)

The sense of loneliness before the moment of awakening. One knows that something is missing in one's life, but one doesn't know exactly what. One may have lived in essential isolation from the world at large, with a sense that one is "not of this time, not of this place."

The sudden and surprising nature of the opening when it occurs.

The feeling that one is now a "new being," whose transformed state is not perceived by the world, including one's closest associates. One appears to be the "old self," but in fact one is a "new self" in disguise.

The feeling that one has been granted a gift one has not earned. One asks, "How could this happen to me, of all people?"

The deep sense of anguish when the Beloved seems to disappear from one's daily life. Underhill says this is the true dark night of the soul. The saint who has known the presence of god suffers even more when that presence is withdrawn.

The sense that one is somehow unworthy, confirmed when the process appears to fade, even temporarily. It is as though one has been tried, and found wanting. (But in fact it almost always begins again.)

The difficulty of expressing such ineffable experience in words. How can you adequately articulate the indescribable?

Questioning whether one is indeed undergoing authentic spiritual transformation or whether one is the victim of some abnormal biological or neural imbalance. (Am I awakened or deluded?)

Discovering that one has no personal control over the experience, which may return only after one has ceased to strive for its presence.

Deep hesitation over sharing such intimate and unfamiliar experience with others. How could anyone else possibly understand? Further, such revelation might seem to diminish the sacred nature of the encounter, or, worse, appear as some form of "bragging" or ego inflation.

A sense that Kundalini is itself a form of consciousness, one which seems to control the experience, now manifesting, now withdrawing, as if to give the initiate time to rest before the next move forward.

The sense that one's own experience is part of a larger process of universal change, planetary initiation, whose ends and purpose no one knows.

HOW BLISS FEELS: ANOTHER ATTEMPT TO DESCRIBE THE INEFFABLE

This morning again it felt as though my practice began before I started. What happened is this: recently I visited a wonderful crystal shop in a small city nestled at the foot of the mountains. I had decided to explore crystals more fully, so I chose two pairs, one of lovely medium size amethyst, the other a small obsidian (manufactured), both shaped into arrowheads. I placed them into a small medicine bag, and once home, I removed them to see what energies I might sense.

At the very instant I held the arrowheads in my hands, I felt delightful sensations flowing freely within. And so I stood there (not yet dressed) clasping them, each time sensing the sweet bliss currents in my subtle (and thus physical) body. I noted particularly the sensations in the lower chakras and upper thighs, as well as the hipbones themselves, and this response pleased me, for these days I experience the delight primarily in the upper body and wish to be more "grounded."

Then I moved my hands up, opening the chakras with this distant movement (never touching my physical body), until I reached my head. And then my "aura" (bliss field) seemed to stretch as far as my arms could reach, always awakening sensuous rapture. Finally, I arrived at the highest point I could reach, just above the center of my crown. And there I found a very delicate point, which I sensed as a "bliss center." I enjoyed this sweet sensation for some time. Indeed, it even seemed to stimulate my eyes (optic nerve? pineal gland?).

And here is the notion that came to me: when our energy body first opens, the intensity resembles the vibrations of a struck Tibetan bowl, and we resonate profoundly with these frequencies that move out in circles, like a stone dropped in water. These frequencies are highly charged, and we experience them as something almost erotic in their impact. Over time, we experience the increasingly softer outer circles, until, finally, we arrive at what seems to be the very outer edge of the energy wave, and these affect us in a much more subtle way, more like gentle light playing over the body. But each emanation is beautiful, each carries its own signature, and each level transforms us until we are ready to move to the next stage. The process never ends.

I feel that these intervals are not merely personal experiences of delightful sensations. I look on them as offerings we make to the planet itself and the cosmos beyond, as we all join in the process of moving together to a higher vibration, cell by cell, person by person, until all are lifted up. And at the end of each such session, we offer prayers for those among us who are in special need, because of pain or illness in their lives.

Her primary feature
is that she is unpredictable.

Fickle suitor,
sometimes She enters
by cheek or brow,
sometimes by hands,
and again in the chakras,
high or low.

She is like a lover
who slips up behind
and gives you a kiss
on your neck
before you know who is
there.

Sometimes
She is waiting
when you wake up
ready to enfold you
in Her arms.

Always, when She beckons,
you come.

part 2

CHALLENGES AND TRIGGERS

WHAT TRIGGERS KUNDALINI?

Apparently, any and everything can bring about a Kundalini awakening. Some study with gurus and teachers and apparently their energies are aroused through the practices they learn. Others, however, undergo seemingly spontaneous awakening experiences, for no obvious reason.

Sometimes personal crisis (of relationship, economic distress, health, for example) can trigger awakening. Other times, the cause is even less evident. One friend "went off" during a visit to Machu Picchu, a trip that was obviously very exciting to her. Another experienced awakening during a spiritual workshop. Another was aroused by a guru who gave her Shaktipat many years ago. Her energies then lay dormant for several decades, but recently she is undergoing energetic transformation in the form of blissful energies.

Recently I heard from two "awakened" writers—one woman had had her energies opened after taking a familiar homeopathic remedy. Another suddenly fell into a Kundalini syndrome (shaking, fear) unexpectedly at her chiropractor's office.

When I first was opened to Kundalini, I was told that I would lose interest in whatever had held my attention before. I thought this was nonsense, but soon I realized I no longer wished to be merely a professor of English literature, but rather to focus primarily on spiritual transformation. I no longer wished to read novels—life itself proved much more interesting. (I did, however, find ways to include material on "new consciousness" in other courses I devised.)

And others have parallel experiences. One psychic who had for years been able to communicate with the dead found she could no longer do this (at least not immediately after her inner shift.) Another "experiencer," from the world of business and other commercial areas, relinquished that avenue for a career in healing.

I think what we discover is this: we are in fact called to serve in whatever way our gifts allow. We restructure our lives to achieve this goal, knowing that we are each, in our own way, part of the larger process, and though we cannot fully describe it, we are certain we are moving in the right direction.

And we feel extremely fortunate to be part of this process. As another friend commented: "It's the only game in town."

QUESTIONS ON KUNDALINI

Here are some questions I have been asked on Kundalini:

1. Is Kundalini an orgasm, or something like an orgasm?

My own answer is no to the first, and maybe to the second. However, Kundalini affects different people in different ways. Some report intense sexual arousal, others lose interest entirely. It has (for me) no sexual provocation, nor a sexual outcome. In fact, sometimes the blissful experience seems to include virtually every part of the body but the lower chakras. How can there be an orgasm if the sexual centers are not involved, and there is no sense of the root or genitals awakening? Then one wonders, where is the energy coming from if not the root? But it is definitely delightful and sensuous. The orgasm or else a pre-orgasmic state is perhaps the nearest thing in human experience to compare it with. It is as though the entire nervous system were awakened in waves of sensuous bliss, which may be gentle or quite intense.

2. Is the experience always the same?

Never. It varies remarkably, just as one's experience of anything (music, sex, viewing a painting, etc.) is never the same. Sometimes the energy flows from the crown downward, sometimes from the root upward, sometimes it is very strong ("like a brass band") and sometimes it is delicate ("a flute playing in the distance"). It has a million guises and disguises, and varies not only from person to person but from time to time.

3. Is it a "nothing but" an experience?

Those who seek to reduce the full visitation to a "nothing but a stirring of chi from breath or meditation or whatever" and who imagine they have had a similar experience which they can easily explain ("it was only…") haven't had it. It is the descent of the Holy Ghost (sacred divine) in such a way that it catapults one into a new reality, and totally transforms the life. Anything less is a "sip" but not the full cup.

4. What is the purpose of Kundalini transformation?

To divinize the human race, to raise humanity to a new level of vibration, in order to prepare it for its advance to the next level of evolution. We don't know exactly what that state will be, when it will occur, or exactly how it will occur. But this is part of a divine process, and it will be executed by divine intelligence. Our role is to acquiesce, to allow the process to play out in our own bodies, to allow the change to occur "creature by creature, being by being."

5. Why is this phenomenon occurring at this time in history?

Because of the acute world crisis. Crisis triggers transformation. And transformation is needed for survival, the race lifted to a revised state.

6. What awakens the Kundalini flow?

Kundalini can be awakened through a myriad of stimuli—yoga, breath, sexual practice designed for the purpose, music, poetry, art, emotions of all sorts including sadness as well as joy. Its initial arousal can be swift or gradual, through specific intent or accidental triggering. No one knows exactly how to awaken it, nor why it chooses to appear when it does. Most of the descriptions are of an ideal model of awakening (energies proceeding in orderly fashion from chakra to chakra), but in fact almost no actual experience conforms to that model.

7. When we feel the energy of the earth itself, is that Kundalini?

According to some, yes. The Kundalini energies are the life force, the essential dynamic of all that is. So—what flows upwards from the earth is cosmic Kundalini. Sacred sites often are located at places where people have felt the earth energies coming forth from time immemorial. In Ireland, they are often the locations of sacred wells or places of ancient gatherings as at Tara, once the place where the kings of Ireland were crowned, and before that the seat of the Great Mother goddess.

8. How widespread is the Kundalini phenomenon at this time?

Again, no one knows for sure. Not so many years ago, few had heard of

Kundalini, much less experienced it, especially in the West. Now there are countless reports of personal experience, many books, web sites, talk sites, seminars, Kundalini yoga centers and so forth. Kundalini consciousness is growing at an increasingly rapid rate, as if humanity as a whole were approaching a point of critical mass, when planetary initiation will occur.

In the mid-nineties, when the Internet was quite new, the word Kundalini brought up a total of four responses. When you Google that word today, you get 11,600,000 results, all in less than one minute. Nonetheless, it is often difficult for the beginning student to locate a qualified and trustworthy teacher or guide.

It is also true that we are facing a world crisis of unimaginable proportions. It is as if the world that we know is collapsing in its outer forms and being rebuilt from within in a different configuration all at the same time.

9. Is full Kundalini awakening evidence of "enlightenment?"

Enlightenment is a state often talked about and seldom achieved. To go through profound Kundalini arousal may take one into a temporary "enlightenment state." It may offer a glimpse or taste of the full enlightenment experience. Certain initiates even claim that they are enlightened. However, I wonder if one in complete and sustained Samadhi wouldn't by that very fact become almost totally disconnected from "this world" and its activities and thus by definition be unable to assist the world in a meaningful way as it strives to navigate these troubled times.

Is it enough to know that "we" are unreal, that we are mere phantoms of our own imagining? Is the person truly enlightened whose private behavior is exploitive of or dishonoring toward others? Isn't something lacking in a guru who knows only a certain technique passed down by his or her own teacher, but cannot converse on matters such as art, or literature or contemporary global issues or Western philosophy or politics? Do we really need "enlightened" beings here at this moment of history, or do we rather need "bodhisattvas" to aid us all in these most desperate times? The latter is of the world, but not in it. She puts her personal salvation to one side, in order to attend to the immediate challenges of humanity and our planet.

The ideal is saint and seer, contemplative and activist, one whose background embraces familiarity with both Western culture and Eastern practices, left brain and right, compassion and commitment. In my view, there may be hidden saints among us, but those persons who openly claim to be enlightened often aren't.

Many of us long for an awakening experience and then find, when it finally happens, that we are having many difficulties dealing with it. Kundalini is fickle. It can bring bliss one day, pain the next. Or it can bring one or the other consistently. It can arouse an array of strange symptoms, both good and bad. It does little good to read about the bliss of the saints or a few other lucky souls, if your body is jerking uncontrollably, your face is twitching, if you are having sudden unpleasant rushes of energy, both hot and cold or other strange "symptoms."

Here are some suggestions for what to do when Kundalini manifests in your body.

1. First and foremost, try to locate a qualified teacher or therapist to help you through. Kundalini awakening is a deeply transformative process, and it is very difficult to make the journey alone. However, finding the right helper may be quite difficult. Try to locate a Transpersonal Therapist who knows what Kundalini is and understands spiritual transformation. You are not just undergoing extreme adjustment of your nervous system and physiology, you are (whether you know it or not) experiencing a profound spiritual awakening, for you are getting in touch with Source at its deepest level—you are discovering that in a very literal sense you and It are one. It is especially important to clear up as much of your psychological baggage as possible. In other words, it is time to clean up your house and get rid of what no longer serves you. Issues long repressed may come to the surface now, and by facing them you can make greater progress in your journey to greater mental health and stability.

2. Since this process is happening in your body, do everything you can to make your physical system stronger. This includes diet, exercise, supplements—anything that will give you a higher level of physical well being. Walking can be very, very helpful—it lets out the built up tension in your system and helps you relax. But do whatever exercise seems best for you.

3. Find a "spiritual buddy" to talk to, preferably someone also

experiencing Kundalini awakening. You need a friend to share this sometimes weird and tumultuous journey with. Talking helps. If you can't find such a friend, at least keep a journal. It will record your progress and you will be able to look back later and recall what the experience of awakening was like in its various stages.

4. Rid your life of as much stress as you can. The more stress, the greater the blockages and possible pain. Find ways to relax—whether from warm baths, or breathing exercises (I like slow in-breath with mouth closed, out-breath with mouth open—it is simple but it does wonders), or chi gong and tai chi, or dancing or just listening to music or saying a mantra or whatever works for you. Slow down. You've got the rest of your life to deal with this major turning point. Allow the inner guide to lead you through.

5. Meditation is good, but I am not convinced that merely sitting on a cushion and trying to clear the mind is the best choice for Kundalini folks. We need to move—and such things as chi gong, or yoga, or dancing, or other physical forms of meditation (and these are meditations themselves) may be more appropriate. Do mantras (sacred phrases) or mudras (sacred hand or bodily gestures) if they help, but don't force yourself to do these if they make you uncomfortable.

6. Whatever you do, don't try to stop the flow of the energies. This can bring about major difficulties. Kundalini has come to you as a gift from the elsewhere—don't refuse the gift, and don't try to dam the flowing stream of energies.

7. Read whatever you like, but don't believe everything you read in books, particularly those texts that rely primarily on ancient writings and techniques. The yogis of earlier times were intently focused on bringing up the energies through the major channels in the body (called Sushumna—the central axis along the spine—plus Ida and Pingala on each side). These latter wind around the Sushumna like the snakes in the medical depiction of the Caduceus. The rising Kundalini often moves through these channels, but it can also manifest through other ways of expression. Sometimes it is a diffuse energy playing through various parts of the body—and can include surprising areas, such as your ears or cheeks or flanks or toes or just about any place it chooses to go. It can be felt in these places as bliss currents or the opposite, depending on where

you are in your process.

Still, there is much good information in books, and it can be reassuring to discover that many others have undergone a process similar to your own. Use your own judgment as to what information is useful to you, what not.

8. If you wish to follow a prescribed technique or method, monitor it to see if it really works for you. I personally feel that we each have an "inner guru" and that it is best to allow it to lead us rather than trying to control it. If a technique is not working (if it makes you feel worse rather than better), drop it, even if some "authority" insists that this is the best approach to Kundalini. Especially in the early stages, it is sometimes better to avoid those practices that arouse more Kundalini energies (such as yoga), though these techniques may be quite useful later when your own energies have settled down more.

9. Don't get too carried away by what is going on with you. Some people think that when their Kundalini opens they are "enlightened" or have been transformed into some kind of spiritual savior. Yes, you are indeed undergoing a very deep transformation, and you will never return to your previous state of "unknowing." But keep a cool head, go about your daily business, and know that "god is on your side." What you are experiencing is a form of divine love available to all humans willing to open to it. Your job is to allow it to fulfill its own purpose, to witness what is happening, and do all you can to integrate and ground the experience.

10. Do pursue grounding techniques to help you through the difficulties that may come up. Grounding might be simple hip rotation, reading a favorite spiritual poem or chapter, being with another person who is herself well "balanced," talking with a spiritual guide or mentor—again, it is a matter of "whatever works for you." Some people change their diets during this phase, becoming vegetarians; others feel that they become more "grounded" by eating hamburger or other heavier dishes. (But stay away from fast foods, too many sweets, alcohol, nicotine, caffeine and such—these will keep you ungrounded for sure.)

11. You may recall past lives, have "weird experiences" such as smelling wondrous odors, hearing beautiful inner music, feel rapture beyond

what you have ever imagined. You may see auras, feel in your own body the energies of others or even inanimate objects. The world may take on an indescribable beauty, and you may sense a compelling "oneness" with everyone and every thing you encounter. You may also have some less pleasant "symptoms" such as those mentioned above—all are part of the process of awakening and adjustment that you are undergoing at this time. You are literally being "made new." These phenomena are all part of the "expansion of consciousness" that comes with the awakening process. They do not mean that you have gone crazy. Many have experienced such transitions to a more open awareness, from ancient times to the present.

12. Find your spiritual center and connect with it daily. Know that you have been given a precious gift, one that will lead you to the deepest possible connection with the Divine. You are receiving divine love in its most vivid expression. You are part of a process now occurring worldwide, all part of the evolutionary shift now occurring for humanity at large as we enter our next stage of consciousness. Now is the time to "invite the divine into your house." Whatever you call it, however you connect with it, "It" has now arrived and is giving you unmistakable signs of its presence and your enduring connection with boundless love.

DRY SPELLS

What are we to do when the initial blaze dies down, when the original emblems and pictures—of the gods and goddesses, the secret images implanted in the chakras—no longer stir us within? We no longer want to turn about and feel the secret currents flow. We scan the sacred texts that so fascinated us early on and find the magic has fled.

We wonder and ask, Is it over? Is the process finished at last? Am I now to be dropped back into the world of the ordinary, the mundane realm where others abide all unaware of the enchanted regions where I have discovered such intense passion and joy?

Today I had these questions and here is the answer that came to me:

I took down a wonderful collection of spiritual writings and on the very first pages found these words:

"All journeys have a secret destination of which the traveler is unaware." (Martin Buber)

These words brought me back to my own true nature as someone forever captivated by the language of longing, a person enamored of the journey and its secret passageways, somebody alive and grateful for what others had given in such great abundance.

Someone once said to me, "It can't be Christmas every day." But then, maybe it can be, if we just know the right place to look for our presents.

PAIN AND ITS SOURCES

I have talked a great deal about bliss (ecstasy), but I also want to say a bit more about pain. Pain is indeed part of the journey, more or less according to the individual aspirant.

In general, I am free of significant pain, but today I had a surprise. I was hoping to go to an afternoon presentation by a well-known channel from England, who is visiting locally at this time. But as I was getting ready, I realized I had many distress symptoms—slight headache, "iffy" stomach, pins and needles all over, including my eyes and toes. Why am I having this reaction? I wondered. This is how I often felt at the beginning of my journey. Haven't I gotten rid of these yet?

And then I realized that somewhere, down very deep, in the forgotten corners of my psyche, I had some apprehension about attending this meeting. I was having unmistakable anxiety symptoms—and then I realized that somehow I was connecting this "channel" with an event that happened years ago when I went to hear another channel (this one now quite famous). When I came home, my house had a strange unpleasant odor, a moldy smell, and I recalled that those who experience (presumably) visits from aliens often describe such an odor. Had I somehow picked up an unwelcome visitor from the session? Was I being plagued by unwelcome guests?

In a few days, the odor disappeared, much to my relief, and it never occurred again. (And I never attended another "channeling.") I think it was this hidden fear that was causing my physical upset, as if my subconscious mind were telling me not to go.

So—I went out for a walk by the city creek instead. It felt good to be out in the fresh air and to see the snow bordering the rushing water. After about forty-five minutes I stopped for a delicious bowl of soup at the local Whole Foods market and then walked back home. By the time I got back, my "symptoms" were gone. Once more, I was reminded how subtle the connections are, and how something not even in the conscious mind can affect our current reactions.

I was also reminded that when the inner energy conduits are not clear, when we have tension and unspoken fear or anxiety, we can find ourselves in pain for sure. I think the trick is to discover the hidden causes and flush them out in any way we can.

But—the channel Solara An-Ra does have an amazing YouTube presentation of a Kundalini exercise. Its music will set the energies moving in bliss, and I did love listening to it as the sweet energies pulsed through my body.
http://www.YouTube.com/user/SolaraAnRa

P. S. After writing the above, I listened to two of Solara An-Ra's actual channelings offered on the same YouTube site. I do not know whether or not she in fact brings in presences from other planetary systems (Sirius or Andromeda), but what she says makes sense and is in fact in line with what many of us are familiar with and indeed believe—we are going through a great earth transition, we are moving into a higher plane of existence, and—for certain—our vibrations are being raised to a new level.

Here is a poem I wrote many years ago, whose thoughts are in line with her presentation:

WAITING

The jeweled cloud sways overhead,
waiting.
Meanwhile our cells are turning
to air,
finer and finer arrangements
of light.

(from *Marrow of Flame*;
now included in *Some Kiss We Want, Poems Selected and New, Second Edition*)

THE SIGNS AND SYMPTOMS
OF KUNDALINI AWAKENING:
LAWRENCE EDWARDS, PH.D.

The following is from Lawrence Edwards, Ph.D.. Lawrence trained as a monk with Muktananda in both India and the US, and wrote his doctoral dissertation on Kundalini. He is a highly respected Jungian therapist who frequently counsels those undergoing Kundalini awakening and/or spiritual transformation. He is also an expert in biofeedback and founded Anam Cara, through which he offers workshops as well as personal observation and counsel. He is an invaluable resource for the Kundalini community.

What are the signs and symptoms of a Kundalini Awakening (KA)?

For countless centuries Kundalini awakening has been viewed by yogis as the greatest blessing and the esoteric goal of all forms of yoga—hatha yoga, mantra yoga, laya yoga, raja yoga, etc. To understand the range of possible experiences that go with Kundalini's blessings it is important to remember from the outset that Her domain encompasses all mental and physical types of experience and all transpersonal and transcendent types of experience as well. Every dimension of our lives can reflect activity, called kriyas—movements of Shakti, the awakened energy of Kundalini—and many dimensions of experience that transcend ordinary waking, dream and deep sleep states of consciousness and ego-bound awareness. Ordinarily all of our experiences fit within the categories or waking, dream and deep sleep— the ordinary states of consciousness in which ego awareness, defined by identification with mind/body and the roles and relationships it inhabits, operates on some level. Thus we think of ourselves as awake or asleep, a man or woman, husband or wife, son or daughter, blue collar or white collar worker, etc., etc., as we identify with various aspects of the mind and body functioning in the world. All of which are ephemeral and reveal only tiny, fractured reflections of our true Self, like shards of a broken mirror reflecting a few brilliant rays of the sun. The Buddha said "as we think, so we become." By identifying with the containers of consciousness—the mind and body—we have the experience of being those containers with all their limitations, suffering, desires, etc.

Kundalini is the power of the Self to know its Self in complete unity consciousness and transform these vehicles of Consciousness, the mind and body, to be capable of manifesting more than just limited ego awareness and lower instinctual brain impulses. In that process of awakening and transformation Kundalini runs Shakti—the power of pure Consciousness— through all the systems of the subtle body and physical body, healing, purifying, expanding, breaking through blockages and burning through karmas. Because each individual differs in their karmic make up, the subtle impressions, the samskaras, being worked on by the Shakti through kriyas, each individual will have their own unique experiences. To blame Kundalini for what karmas and samskaras our physical and subtle bodies contain is another game of the mind trying to avoid responsibility for the consequences of its actions—past and present.

Physical kriyas include shaking, trembling, involuntary movements, sensations of heat or cold, horripilation, spontaneous hatha yoga postures, spontaneous alterations in breathing—pranayama, rushes of energy, rushes of sensual/sexual/orgasmic energy, stimulation of sex organs and orgasms, cessation of sexual desire or interest, loss of appetite, food cravings, tingling sensations, sparking/electricity sensations, the feeling of ants crawling all over one's skin, roaring like a lion, spontaneous sounds chanted or spoken aloud, spontaneous mudras and dance-like movements, gentle swaying during meditation, rocking back and forth, heart racing or pounding, breathing coming to a full stop and staying still, and more and more. People write poetry, sing, dance, paint, draw, create in new and never-before expressed ways, all inspired by Kundalini's grace. The gentle movements, breath alterations, rushes of energy, feeling of heat and cold, tingling, sounds and mantras, and sexual stimulation are most common, along with euphoric, blissful feelings and expansive states of love and unity awareness.

Each of our senses can manifest the movements of Kundalini. There are visions, colors, blue pearls and every conceivable archetypal form to be seen. There are divine scents, exquisite sounds, super sensuous touch, and ambrosial tastes to be experienced as gift of Shri Kundalini.

There are also very rare but notable instances of people getting rashes, diarrhea, and various painful conditions, food sensitivities or allergies, and the manifestation of latent, karmicly held diseases or disorders now surfacing to be released.

Kundalini works to free our consciousness from polarities, including bondage to attraction and aversion. So regardless of what comes up in the process of Kundalini sadhana, one practices the inner posture of detached awareness, watching, witnessing, neither pursuing nor avoiding.

Every form of emotion and mental event can also be manifested as kriyas. One can laugh, cry, go into ecstasy, grief, fury, bliss, etc. etc. As with all kriyas, these are viewed with the detachment of Witness Consciousness, neither pursuing nor avoiding what is arising. NONE OF THESE EXPERIENCES IS THE GOAL. THEY ARE SCENERY ALONG THE WAY, GIFTS OF THE SHAKTI TO BE APPRECIATED AND RECEIVED FOR WHAT THEY REVEAL, BUT NOT TO DISTRACT ONE FROM THE GOAL. As long as there is an experience and an experiencer, i.e., an object and a subject, one is in a lower state of duality, no matter how alluring that experience may be. These experiences have a very real danger of inflating the ego as it attempts to possess them and identify with them. For this reason spiritual traditions have practices for keeping the ego deflated and grounded, which is part of the role of the teacher/guru/master, as well as teachings about not becoming overly fascinated by various transcendent phenomena.

ANY KRIYA, PHYSICAL OR MENTAL/EMOTIONAL, THAT MAY HAVE MEDICAL, NEUROLOGICAL OR PSYCHIATRIC SIGNIFICANCE SHOULD BE CHECKED OUT BY THE APPROPRIATE HEALTH CARE PROFESSIONALS. I've seen cases where someone dismissed a symptom as a kriya and it turned out to the symptom of a medical or psychiatric disorder like high blood pressure, diabetes, bipolar disorder, etc. It's always worth having such things checked out medically even if it is only to rule out a possible problem.

To begin with read: Swami Muktananda: Play of Consciousness; Swami Tirtha: Devatma Shakti; Sir John Woodroffe: Serpent Power; Lawrence Edwards: The Soul's Journey www.thesoulsjourney.com;
Dorothy Walters: Unmasking the Rose: A Record of a Kundalini Initiation; and there's also a reading list on www.thesoulsjourney.com.

MORE ON BLISS AND PAIN

A question we often ask ourselves is this: What indeed is the relationship between bliss and pain?

And first we wonder "What is bliss?"

There are as many kinds and states of bliss as there are people, and their own myriad states of consciousness. I tend to think of two major kinds of bliss: somatic and non-somatic. The former includes a clearly perceived bodily state of sensuous feeling, which one person described as "like sex only different." It may have, but need not have, a sexual origin, and may have, but need not have, a sexual goal. Some people take modern day "tantric workshops" to bring more feeling into their sexual relationships. Some people dedicate their bliss feelings to the divine itself, which seems to flow through the body in states of heightened awareness and hence is thought of as the "Beloved Within." And some tantrics (Baba Hari Dass is one) practice strict forms of celibacy and view bliss states as something to "go beyond."

There are also certain states of consciousness which some people call "bliss" that in fact are more like "trancing out."

Often people use the term "bliss" to refer to delight or tranquility or good feelings or pleasure. It is a very tricky word, with many overlapping categories and overtones. It is like all subjective states, capable of myriad definitions and gradations of meaning.

When a person is suddenly flooded with Kundalini rapture (that is, he or she is being "opened" in a very mysterious process), she is like a new born babe, and needs special care. The nervous system is being radically reconstructed, and she is suddenly thrust into a world where things look, feel, and sound different from anything she has known before. For a time, she needs to be freed from the demands of ordinary living. If possible, she should go into some form of seclusion surrounded by sympathetic aides and helpers, who will care for her tenderly during this initial period.

Alas, most people do not have access to this kind of privileged care. They must make it on their own, deal with the utterly new and dazzling sensations, and cope as best they can with the swings of mood and emotions that may follow.

This state of transition is not easy. Even bliss is sometimes hard to bear (because of its unfamiliarity and intensity.) Many times, there is no one to share with, no one even to talk to. And the bliss may be followed (sooner or later) by acute pain, either over long periods of time or else in briefer interludes.

So—I think anyone in this state must be excused (for the time being) from too much concern for the troubles of the world and focus on the intense inner process which is going on within.

How long does this "state of emergence" last? As long as it takes. But, as time goes by, the bliss states often become less frequent, and the pain (if it occurs) less intense, and one can begin, gradually to enter the world again.

In these early days, one can be so open that she picks up the pain in another's body, feeling it as her own. Some seem to experience the pain and agony of the world at large as their own.

At some point, one is ready to turn awareness once more to the challenges and problems and pain of the surrounding society. One can then follow various paths of "giving back," finding ways to help others cope with pain or to encourage them on their own paths. Some are able to use the blissful energies as healing forces for others. I longed to become an energy healer, but discovered that I was too sensitive to do so—I simply mirrored the other's pain in my body, and so we had two people in distress instead of one. I can still pick up on others' feelings, whether good or bad—frequently I get a "hit" in my body, sometimes just from strangers walking by.

I have hoped that my writings have been helpful to others coming along. I have focused on the "bliss" part of the journey, because it seemed to me that that was the great discovery, at least for me—that we, in our bodies, could open in unsuspected ways to great ecstasy in addition to pain. Many people say this blissful state is in fact the "natural" condition of our existence, and that society has programmed it out of us. Some say it is our birthright.

I have also felt it was important to stress the positive features of the body awakening to bliss because the patriarchy has so long denied women the right to claim such feelings as part of their natural heritage. The body in many cultures and societies (our own included) has often been reviled, rejected, humiliated—we all are familiar with the record. Part of the process of healing for all women (and some men) is to come into a state of acceptance of the fact that bodily pleasure (including but not confined to sex) is OK, that it is alright to feel good, to acknowledge and accept this wondrous inner state as a token of the divine connection.

In my case, part of the great discovery was that pleasurable bodily sensations were not specifically connected to sex, but rather to the joyful dance of the atoms inside. Music has been very important in this regard.

So—when I do my meditation practice, I offer it to the world of all sentient beings, asking that all may be blessed and healed. I usually include prayers for those I know personally who are suffering or facing great challenges, and then ask that healing occur in the world at large. My practice sometimes includes bliss states, sometimes not. I have, for the most part, moved into a new stage of my life where the somatic states are less pronounced. But when the bliss currents were strong, I did not try to stop them, because that would have been a disaster. But now I do not mourn their absence—I simply accept that which comes as right for me, and welcome them when they occasionally reappear.

And I am extremely concerned about the fate of the world. I find that many of my friends are, as I am, greatly disturbed by current world events. Like me, they fear for the future of our country and for the world. I think the whole global scene is a tinderbox sitting on a pile of kindling ready to explode, and that our leaders are like children playing with matches with little awareness of the consequences of their acts.

Knowing that bliss is a possibility for the human state offers great comfort and reassurance. It tells me the divine is present in our world, in the face of all darkness. It reminds me of the place from which we have come, and to which we will return at death. It is the kiss of the goddess that sustains us as we go. The divine embrace is holding us as we enter into what I believe is a new stage of human evolution, despite all the signs of societal failure. We are being devastated and redeemed all at the same time. I think current chaos is part of the transition to a new vibration, and we are now learning to live in it.

If one had to choose between bliss feelings and compassionate action, of course one would choose the latter. But my ideal is both, bliss to give us courage and strength and to affirm our divine origins and connection, and compassionate action to fulfill our core commitment to the world.

This is a place you enter
without key or combination.
It is where your spirit lives
when you are out
doing errands
or at the theater with friends.

It is always waiting,
like a constant lover,
a devoted friend.

It keeps changing
how it looks,
becomes a shape shifter,
a floating image
in the trees.

But when you find it again,
its face is always familiar,
like the one you looked
at so carefully
after you were born.

Sometimes it is a rose garden,
sometimes a temple,
sometimes the rose itself
unfolding.

TERESA'S ANGEL

Sometimes I think
it might have been easier,
not to have been touched
by that stroke of fire,
not to have been consumed,
like Moses' bush, by that
flame that does not burn,
nor to have been lifted
to those storied heavens
where the gods look down
and never speak.

What does it mean
to die
before death comes?
To arrive when the journey
has barely just begun?

How would life have been
infused with the ordinary,
days worn thin with repetition,
children crying in the night,
bread rising, the wine jug filled,
as if by doing again and again
one might progress toward
an unknown goal?

On the chapel wall,
god stretches out his hand

to Adam,
and Adam comes alive,
ready to be born once more.

How did you greet
that angel who arrived?
How did you bear it,
that shock of light,
when god entered every cell?

Saint Teresa, who lived in the sixteenth century, was noted for her "raptures." Although no one can say for certain what these were, I believe she was experiencing what we today would call "Kundalini bliss," divine union through ecstatic states of awareness.

The sculptor Bernini did a famous piece showing Teresa of Avila in full ecstasy, her face transfigured in joy as the angel beside her pierces her heart with his lance. This is her moment of awakening, her transition into overwhelming bliss.

In many ways, her experience resembles that of those awakened by Kundalini, whose intensity at times threatens to overwhelm. Though we delight in this new found state of boundless love, some of us also may question from time to time if this is what we really want, for the blessing comes at a price. Teresa herself suffered recurrent illness during her transformation process.

Teresa's most famous book is called "The Interior Castle." It maps the stages of spiritual progress to god. I think that many "K-ers" also live in an "interior castle," for we frequently find it difficult or impossible to share our inner experiences with others.

KUNDALINI AND THE BRIDAL NIGHT

No doubt about it, Kundalini is like a marriage. First comes the ceremony (the preparation) followed by the night of love. This is the bridal night, the time of discovery, of intense, unbearable bliss (and some pain as the old spirit is relinquished), and continuous, wild inner celebration. At last, the inner voice says, I have found it. Finally, I have arrived at my true destination, the home I have dreamed about, the lost Eden I have sought for so long.

The world without wears a face of luminous beauty. Everyone and everything is exquisitely lovely. All of humanity reflects the perfection of the divine, and there is no separation between the self and others.

And the ecstasy, the lovemaking, continues unabated for days, for weeks, months even. It is said that some never return to their prior state, but remain always wafted onto another plane, somewhere beyond the merely human.

Then one day, there is an interruption. Something doesn't feel right. There is pain, unease, a general sense of malaise. One senses that this is not a perfect union after all. Bride and groom discover they are not an ideal match, the house is too small to accommodate two such separate beings. There are differences—and the newlyweds realize they are not really a single entity, but dual selves who have cast their lot together, made eternal promises they can never undo. And, in the case of Kundalini, it is as if two individual consciousnesses, two very different natures, are trying to occupy the single house of one body/psyche, trying to meld themselves together into a wholeness, each striving to merge with a stranger.

And from this point on, the struggle continues. Along with the pain, the suffering, are nights of utter euphoria, days of unimaginable transcendent bliss. But, sooner or later, ecstasy is again replaced by suffering, anguish takes the place of joy, and one wonders what sort of bargain has been struck.

And so it continues, month after month, year after year, until at last the warring partners make peace, each having given up something of value, each having received some priceless treasure in return. The merely human has surrendered a major portion of ego in order to know this unsuspected reality. The energies which emanate from the "higher" source as Kundalini have entered and transformed matter, but this physical home lacks many of the freedoms of the totally discarnate state. It learns not to call upon its partner so often, to respect the limits of the other. And like a fickle lover, it sometimes disappears without warning, seems to abandon altogether the faithful spouse left waiting behind, wondering what has changed.

But, somehow, the energies always return, manage through now familiar paths of seduction to enjoy once more the good graces of the ever-forgiving partner. And after a difficult and seemingly endless process, they are finally fused together, they are indeed a New Being. They are ready to set forth, to become visible to the world and reveal the results of this arduous alchemy, the human not perfected but indelibly transformed.

BETROTHED

So at the end of the day, we give thanks
for being betrothed to the unknown . . .
—John O'Donohue

However one looks at it,
it was not easy—
that bridal night,
mingling of self
and the unknown who appeared.

Everything took place
in secrecy and silence,
at the hidden center,
the core where presence
begins.

How do you mate
with something unseen?
Become one
with what has no form or name?

The days were filled with sweetness
and tumult,
nights so intense
that passion itself
became too pale a word.

The world unfolded

in endless celebration,
a constant feast to which
the heart said yes,
the spirit yearned.

Now, old lovers,
we live quietly,
sometimes meet
and nod in recognition,
remembrance of that special time,
when we no longer knew
who was lover, who beloved.

(from *Some Kiss We Want: Poems Selected and New*)

GOING THROUGH KUNDALINI ALONE

Going through Kundalini alone is one of the greatest of life's challenges. One longs for an "expert," someone who can answer our questions, give us advice and guidance, and in general serve as a sympathetic ear for us in this most momentous experience.

Unfortunately, many lack helpful support, even today, when Kundalini is becoming more and more common around the world. There are, of course, many internet Kundalini sites. But there is no readily available list of groups meeting locally or regionally, few lists of qualified therapists or listeners. The Kundalini Research Network meets from time to time and offers helpful suggestions on its website. My advice, always, is to try to find at least one person who is willing to become your "spiritual buddy," with whom you can share your intimate experiences. The listener does not have to be undergoing Kundalini themselves, but they should at least be serious spiritual seekers, and they should be able to share freely with you their own adventures on their chosen path. If you can find (and afford) a good transpersonal therapist, he or she can be quite helpful. And (again if you can afford it) methods such as massage or even acupuncture can also help alleviate symptoms (for some).

One thing you can do is to keep a journal. This will be quite helpful in terms of maintaining your own sense of inner development, and will serve you well in future when you can go back to review your progress.

Another possibility is workshops or attendance at presentations of spiritual teachers. Often it is reassuring simply to be in the presence of like-minded souls, and these sessions offer the possibilities of meeting others whose experience is similar in some way to your own.

And, I think it is helpful to follow some simple spiritual practice, either quiet or moving, that will give you a sense of continuity and help to settle the inner unrest. You may also take comfort in reading some of the basic texts on Kundalini, such as Bonnie Greenwell's Energies of Transformation, or Kundalini Rising (a major anthology from Sounds True) or other books you may find just by going to the bookstore or checking out Amazon or the internet. My own "Unmasking the Rose: A Record of a Kundalini Initiation" has helped many. More recently, I have published "The Kundalini Poems: Reflections of Radiance and Joy" and many have found this book inspiring. And—don't forget the site http://www.kundalinisupport.org/ that is one of the most helpful of the various websites.

Overall, time is the best healer, generally bringing relief to unpleasant states and a sense of grounding and balance into your life.

HOW NOT TO MEDITATE

Normandi Ellis, in her marvelous book Awakening Osiris has a memorable sentence: "Some days it is easier to commune with the gods than others."

Today was such a day for me. Usually I do my practice the first thing after I get up, but this morning I needed to check with the apartment manager on something and went downstairs to confer with him. While I was there, I met and talked with other residents of the complex. Then, when I went back to my apartment and started my practice, there was loud talk and the sounds of doors slamming in the hallway (though it is usually extremely quiet here).

The result was that I wasn't able to concentrate very well—the energies were barely discernible. I kept trying music to see if that would help, but nothing seemed to change.

In addition, today is overcast, with high atmospheric pressure, a condition that often creates (for me) sinus pressure, making it even more difficult to see without eyestrain, especially at the computer.

I thought I would report these events lest others imagine that every single day in my life is filled with ecstasy and delight. Actually, I feel fine, but just wanted to add (for the record) that this is "one of those days" when nothing seems to carry you to the heights you have so recently experienced.

Kundalini is mysterious and unpredictable. It must be treasured and nourished carefully to attain the best results.

But of course, we must enter each meditation with "no expectations," and be grateful for the gifts that are granted. With this, as with all other human experiences, it can't be a momentous celebration every day (at least not for most of us).

A HIDDEN WORLD BELOW (IN SAN FRANCISCO)

Today it was the lake once more, again the late afternoon sun gilding the surface of grass and trees, Nora pulling and tugging at the leash. My attention is focused on her and her pranks, so I do not observe my fellow promenaders as closely as before. But I do spot a few mothers pushing their babes, a few elderly folk proceeding cautiously on their canes.

When Nora and I pass the concession stand, we go by the picnic tables on the widened sidewalk nearby. This area is a favorite gathering place for aging Russian émigrés. Nearby is a part of the city that is "their" neighborhood; it even contains an Orthodox Church with an onion dome. Once last summer when I was passing by, a woman (obviously one of the attendants for this group outing from a retirement home) was playing plaintive Russian songs on her accordion, while her elderly charges, some in wheel chairs, listened and nodded. A few even danced in stately dignity to these nostalgic ballads.

Today a small remnant is examining what appears to be a large map (or is it a game board?) spread out over the table. I wonder if it is a map of Russia. Perhaps they are telling stories of their homeland, where they were born, even what life was like for them there. Then I reflect that they would likely have been born around 1920, too young to have fled the country alone. Perhaps their parents got out a few years later. These adults speak Russian, so they must have lived there for at least a few years.

I think about how quickly things can change, how a life that seems settled and fixed can suddenly be turned totally around by some intense and unforeseen happening. And, of course, that makes me think of Kundalini, which so frequently strikes us when we are least expecting it, possibly have not even heard of it. Something unknown seems to control our destiny in its basic outlines. Hence (I think) the futility of making too detailed life plans. There is always a wild card that we cannot read ahead of time.

As we circle along on the western edge of the lake, I realize that something is different here today. The sun is at a low angle, and the pines lining the edge of the little island tucked away in the center are reflected below in the water, swaying and rippling with the current. The water is pristine, clearer than I have ever seen it. The great pine trunks extend both upward and downward, each image mirroring the original in a kind of primal luster. I pause to savor this undulating harmony.

It is as if there is a hidden, underwater world, a secret realm beneath, opened here in this special moment. I am held in semi-trance. I wonder if indeed there are not other such underwater kingdoms, the source of the stories of nymphs and sprites and other nature spirits, who inhabit a fairy realm, one that calls to us when we are least aware. There are many stories of those who were captured and carried away to magic places by such hypnotic beings. Likewise, there are modern tales of UFOs stationed out of sight in bodies of water. Water is mysterious, fascinating, the place of the unknown. I think how easy it would be to linger here indefinitely, lulled by irresistible beauty. Suddenly I know why Narcissus jumped.

And again, my thoughts turn to Kundalini, how those of us who participate in its mysterious stirrings inhabit a world invisible to the majority. We are at once acknowledged residents of the mundane world, and the undetected dwellers of an unknown universe. It is as if we have been called to join a secret society, which others can neither see nor comprehend.

Yes, I could linger here mesmerized by the wavering surface and plangent depths forever, but the light is fading, and I must hurry home. I think of Robert Frost's well-known poem, "Stopping by Woods," with its famous ending lines:

"The woods are lovely, dark, and deep,
But I have promises to keep,
And miles to go before I sleep.
And miles to go before I sleep."

I think the big question is, as always, what is the relationship of such moments of bliss to pain, especially the pain and suffering of others and the world at large.

part 3

SOME MAJOR ISSUES

HOW TO TELL A TRUE TEACHER
FROM A FALSE ONE

1. Trust your gut.

2. Use your head.

3. Anyone who tells you that they are enlightened, isn't.

4. Anyone who claims to have all the answers, doesn't.

5. Look at the "followers." Do they look healthy and happy, or are they depressed, emaciated, listless?

6. Are you invited to explore and compare these teachings with others?

7. Is this a closed system, or one of open inquiry?

8. Does the leader enjoy an overly affluent lifestyle?

9. Does the leader indulge in abuse of the followers—sexual, mental, emotional, even financial?

10. Does the leader engage in egregious commercialism, with the obvious goal of financial gain?

11. Does the teacher honor and respect each person, no matter what their level of spiritual or personal development?

12. Are students punished or threatened with dire consequences for not adhering to a strict regimen and belief system?

13. Does the teacher promise more than anyone could deliver? Is it a "quick road to enlightenment"?

14. Does the teacher listen? Is the teacher willing to be taught?

15. Is the teacher addicted to drugs or alcohol or sex or money?

16. Does the teacher have something of value to offer, something beyond what you (and most others) already know?

17. Is the instruction useful or a waste of your time?

18. Does the teacher expect to be treated more like a god than a fellow journeyer who wishes to share some of his/her gifts with the world?

And—what makes a good teacher? Just the opposite of the above. However, an authentic teacher with valuable insights and direction to offer is quite rare. There are many charlatans abroad, some of whom prey on their students to serve their own ego needs. Others sincerely believe what they put forth, and are simply misguided. Some seem to know little other than what their teacher or tradition handed down to them.

Find someone who makes you think, "I would like to be like that person in some way." Find someone who excites you, who is full of passion, who is sincere and articulate. Find someone who has thought deeply about things, and gives wisdom as a gift. It has been said that the best teacher is one who is slightly more advanced than the student, but not so far ahead that the student cannot follow.

Find someone from whom you can learn. Find someone who is kind. Find someone who is not afraid to love.

DISCIPLINE VS. SPONTANEOUS JOY

I recently spoke with a friend who does two hours of spiritual practice each morning, mostly mantra repetition. When I asked her if she felt the energies move, she said only on a very subtle level. This gentle approach spares the body any discomfort (she explained.)

Then this morning I went to Golden Gate Park (in San Francisco) and for the first time saw the large group of tai chi practitioners who gather there each Sunday morning for two hours. For years I have wanted to visit this class, perhaps to join in, certainly to feel the exquisite energies I was certain must flow there.

What I observed was, to me, more like a military drill. The instructor spoke through a loudspeaker, leading the large crowd through a complex series of intricate postures, one coming on the heels of another, the entire process taking a very long time. The emphasis seemed to be on "getting it right," rather than on "getting in touch with the within."

I was reminded of the time I visited a Zen Center to receive preliminary instruction. When I discovered that the meditation was a carefully controlled ritual, where every movement was prescribed, I realized that this was not for me. I was certain that I would forget and step into the zendo on the wrong foot, or turn to face the wall from the wrong direction. Later we observed the tea ceremony, again a rite conducted under strict protocol.

I myself am not clear as to why people follow such carefully orchestrated procedures to such a degree. Of course, tai chi practice is good for the body, keeping it limber and supple. Quiet meditation does calm and balance the mind. And certain asanas, certain moves of chi gong, certain sounds do indeed awaken the energetic centers and allow for a truly invigorating and often enrapturing experience. But must the approach be so rigid? Must the instructions be followed with such total mechanical precision? Anxiety over "whether I am doing it right" can prevent awareness of inner feelings. Someone even suggested that students obtain satisfaction simply from the act of "mastering" the practice.

Following the precise protocol is, for them, itself the reward. Always, I am wondering, what do they feel, if anything other than the gratification of being able to follow difficult instructions? Many people prefer such regimented modes, so they must gain some benefit. But always I am unclear as to what this might be.

For the person whose Kundalini energies are fully awakened, almost any movement or mantra can produce an exquisite flow of shakti, affirmation of divine connection. Thus some "invent" their own tai chi forms, improvise their own mudras and mantras. These achieve easily and spontaneously what the various energy and sound practices are meant to accomplish. The channels are wide open. The range of energetic response is vast. These responses, whether subtle or intense, are a "self-validating experience," one the practitioner yearns to repeat again and again, not as an imposed discipline but as pure joy in existence itself, confirmation of the divine source of all being.

And, of course, there are also problems with such a seemingly random, inner directed mode. Both the physical and subtle energy bodies can become unbalanced, and produce unwelcome symptoms, such as illness or emotional disturbance. The swings from pleasure to pain can be dramatic, with no apparent cause for either extreme. If the student is not sufficiently grounded, from prior life experience or mental maturity, the experience can lead to a state of disconnection with the "real" world of practical affairs.

But some of us are the "rugged individualists" of the spiritual realm. We test all authority, follow our gut instincts, make our own discoveries as we go. Whether we rush headlong into disaster, or soar into the empyrean, we are our own guides and teachers. We seek the connection to the original source, not the (sometimes) diluted or distorted philosophies and practices often proffered on the contemporary scene. After all, someone had to invent these movements, discover the power of these syllables. My own guess is that the originators felt the effect of the moves quite clearly as bliss within, repeated the mantras because these sacred syllables resonated wondrously within their own bodies. And, for us today, there is still a "teacher within" waiting to reveal the sacred paths if we but pause to attend. We do not avoid all teachings, nor shun all preset directions. But we pick and choose carefully, adopting only those ideas and approaches that feel "right" to us.

MYTHS AND MISCONCEPTIONS ABOUT KUNDALINI

1. Kundalini will awaken only after many years of preparation and effort, including austere diets, purification practices, and mastery of advanced yogic techniques.

Kundalini can awaken suddenly at any stage of spiritual development, including times when the student is apparently totally unprepared. Often it appears to manifest as a token of divine grace, but no one knows why a particular recipient is so blessed. Some believe that unexpected awakenings may be related to the energy body one brings in from past lives.

2. Kundalini is a "snake" that rises up the spine, chakra by chakra, until it —finally, perhaps after years of striving—reaches the crown.

Kundalini may awaken in many ways. It can shoot suddenly from base to crown, or it can appear in various unrelated parts of the body, such as hands, arms, cheeks, brow, or in the lower chakras. It follows its own pathway. Thus each aspirant undergoes a unique pattern of unfolding.

3. Only those especially gifted can experience Kundalini.

Kundalini is the life force of the universe itself. It exists within every living thing (and perhaps within the inanimate realm as well). Thus it lives within each of us. To awaken Kundalini is simply to become conscious of the energies that are already there.

4. Kundalini awakening always brings extreme suffering and bizarre symptoms, such as shaking, involuntary vocalization, headaches, and physical pain.

Often the physical/mental/emotional systems are not prepared to receive the intense spiritual energies now arriving in the body. When blocks occur, difficulties may ensue. In extreme cases, psychotherapy, somatic restructuring, and other forms of expert help may be needed.

Kundalini—once accessed in its pure form—can bestow intense ecstasy or bliss, and thus the recipient feels very blessed, as if he/she were receiving infusions of divine love. Kundalini then exists as bliss-consciousness, as if the goddess herself had entered one's body.

5. The main use of Kundalini is to enhance sexual pleasure.

Although Kundalini may intensify sexual feelings, that is not its primary purpose. It produces—immediately or ultimately—a state of "suprasex," extremely delightful somatic impulses (bliss waves) erotic in tone, but not to be confused with ordinary body based sexual experience. Suprasex is, rather, brought about by the sublimation (transformation to a higher level) of the natural sexual energies, bringing them into a truly spiritual expression, a state that can be accessed well into one's later years. One enjoys the pleasurable nature of such states of consciousness, but one knows that each such episode is a deep encounter with the profoundly sacred for it implies union with the god/goddess. No physical stimulation is included—rather, receptivity and attention are the keys.

Ultimately, no one knows the full truth about Kundalini. It remains part of the Great Mystery which surrounds us and of which we are all a part.

6. The chakras are accurately described by the conventional system of correspondences, with each assigned a particular color, function, and emotions.

Thus the root is connected with survival, the second with sex, the solar plexus with power, the heart with love, the throat with truth, the third eye with psychic ability, and the crown with union and enlightenment (this last is, however, correct, for this is where realization of ultimate truth occurs).

Actually, each chakra functions as a part of a whole, a field of energy with intermeshing parts, all of whom are equal components in a unified system.

7. The chakras awaken in a precise, linear order.

There is not a particular order in which the chakras awaken. They can, in fact, seem to move (awaken) back and forth, now one, now the next, then back again to the former, in no predictable pattern. Crown can open before solar plexus, third eye before heart. The openings seem to occur as directed by an inner consciousness, not as logic might assume.

8. We all have the same number of chakras.

The number as well as the precise location of the chakras may vary from person to person, for each is unique. Some systems count five, others seven, and still others even more.

A MORNING SURPRISE

This morning, as I stood in my dressing room and prepared to brush my teeth and get ready for the day, I decided to try something different. I took a whiff of my favorite essential oil (frankincense and amber) to see if it would offer a moment of relaxation, as it often does. I immediately felt my shoulders go down in a more relaxed pose, but then I felt something more. To my surprise, I began to feel bliss, here and there, in this area and then that. What started as nearly imperceptible joy (stroked gently by a feather?) grew until I was feeling deep delight everywhere I moved my hands (again, never touching). I continued this sweet practice for about thirty minutes, about the maximum time I can easily stand.

This lovely experience led me to contemplate, once more, the difference between asana yoga as sacred practice and yoga as secular exercise. Of course, the latter has many benefits. It revivifies and tones the body in marvelous ways. It gives you more energy, makes you more loving toward your fellows, and makes you stronger and healthier.

But true yoga has none of these as its purpose. The word "yoga" is generally interpreted to mean "yoke" or "joining." But what is yoked or joined? Done with the right attitude, it is the small self uniting with the large Self, human connecting to the divine. To achieve this state, it is essential to have the Kundalini awake and functioning in harmony with the great life force that creates and animates the universe. It is at that point that we know what we truly are—a tiny particle in the Great Bliss that is called god/goddess, the ultimate reality. The corollary of this is the realization that we, in fact, do not exist as separate beings, for It and we are one, in the way a droplet is part of the ocean wave. Many are angry and deeply disappointed at this idea, for in them the "ego" (sense of separate self) is strong. However, I believe that our energetic body (subtle body) survives mortal death, and so we may reappear in new packaging as humans or other astral beings again.

Does what is called "Kundalini yoga" awaken Kundalini? I have my doubts, but have had others who have practiced it claim otherwise. Is "hot yoga" actually yoga or just a form of exercise? Yoga was created in a very hot climate, where I think it was especially suited for slow movements, held for sufficient time to allow one to feel a spiritual connections to the unknown gods. Remember, in ancient times in India and elsewhere there were ceremonies specifically designed to summon the gods. I suspect that their arrival involved not so much a physical manifestation as deep ecstatic feelings within, such as can be known (to some extent) even today through slow and thoughtful movement.

Alas, some yoga teachers today do not even know the history of yoga, its purpose or intended divine nature. They do good in the world, but not that which was the original intention.

One more thought: I believe that the origins of the actual asanas of yoga, as well as the movements of such practices as chi gong or tai chi, came about because the ancient practitioners found that certain bodily postures awakened bliss, and thus these became the favored forms. Today the emphasis is often on doing the forms correctly, not feeling the energies they were created to arouse. Once the movements were codified, they often lost their original shakti and became rituals empty of inner joy. I consider experiences such as I had this morning to be a form of yoga, for they reinforce one's sense of connection to that which is most sacred and most mysterious in human experience. Anything (music, nature, art, poetry) that arouses this feeling is also yoga, the ultimate connection to the unseen divine.

ARE THE CHAKRAS REAL?

Some writers insist that the chakras are not in fact "real" as actual centers of subtle feeling, but are merely abstractions or intellectual conventions. I think these are analysts who have not themselves experienced the wondrous power of the chakras as they awaken in blissful pulsation. If they had even once felt such profound rapture, they would no longer question.

Others want to view the chakras in an ordered hierarchy, from base to crown, sometimes even deprecating the lower chakras as aspects of "the animal nature" which we must strive to transcend. For me, each chakra is a sacred center which god (the goddess/the divine energetic) loves to visit. This energy seems to flow impartially in lower and higher, though it is true we may become aware of the "lower" centers earlier in our development. But none is more or less worthy than another. I think of the chakras like notes on a flute, some higher, some lower, all capable of expanding into luminous beauty.

The primary difference, I believe, is that the energy of the higher chakras draws us closer to pure consciousness, where the distinction between observer and thing observed dissolves. When rapture is awakened in the root, we are well aware that something is happening to some part of "us." At the crown, we and what we are experiencing are merged as one.

Women, in particular, have struggled to recapture their essential connection with the creative earth energies associated with the lower chakras. The right to survive, the right to experience the full joy of the body, the right to assert one's needs before the world—these have been brought into sharp focus in recent years through feminism. (Many yogic systems associate these capacities with the first three chakras.) Likewise the heart that opens to compassion, the throat which pours forth its own artistic expressions, the "third eye" which begets the capacity for intuitive perception—all of these are important segments of the whole.

But the chakra is more than a symbolic expression of a human trait. Each is a place that feels, and such feeling brings awareness of our lost birthright, "bliss consciousness." At the crown, one discovers that one does not exist, after all. The only reality is overwhelming love. In that embrace, the seeker knows at last who she is, the truth of her own being, which is itself a manifestation of divine love.

REFLECTIONS ON THE INNER GURU

A footnote in *Tibetan Yoga and Secret Doctrines* (ed. by W. Y. Evans-Wentz) states:

"It is a fundamental tenet of the Buddhism of all Schools that the human *guru* is merely a guide, as was the Great *Guru*, Gautama the Buddha. Each aspirant for Nirvanic Enlightenment must be a law unto himself; he himself, not the *guru*, must tread the Path. One must eat one's food for oneself; and, as the Buddha taught, each pilgrim on the Great Pilgrimage must really be his own light and his own refuge. Nirvana is to be realized not by the proxy of a *guru*, but by the *yogi* himself."

Elsewhere in the text, this footnote appears:

"When, in virtue of having practiced yogic meditation, there has been established communion between the human mind and the divine mind, or between the normal human consciousness and the super-normal cosmic consciousness, man attains to true understanding of himself. He realizes intuitively that the Knower, and all objects of knowledge, or all knowing, are inseparably a unity; and simultaneously with this realization there is born the Great Symbol, which occultly signifies this spiritual illumination. Like a philosopher's stone, the Great Symbol purges from the mind the dross of Ignorance (Avidya); and the human is transmuted into the divine by the spiritual alchemy of *yoga*."

ABOUT ANGELS AND REINCARNATION

All of us wonder, from time to time, about the question of reincarnation. Have we (or some form of what we think of as ourselves) lived before, in some other time period, some other place? Occasionally, we get echoes—some feeling of déjà vu (I've been here, done this, experienced this before)—or are stirred by what seems like inner recollection.

Another question that arises often is, Where does the sudden explosion of ecstatic Kundalini within the slumbering self come from if not some prior existence? How can someone, previously ignorant of the subtle energies and all their latent powers, unexpectedly be flooded with bliss, opened by unknown forces to a rapture she had never before suspected?

In the video version of Angels in America there are two brilliant scenes in which an angel appears, descending in splendor to embrace the human in expansive divine love. This love is physical as well as "spiritual." It is felt as well as perceived. It is real, it is powerful, it is undeniable. It is the ultimate union of human and divine, leaving its earthly subjects astonished and transformed.

In the script of this powerful drama, the option is left open to interpret these heavenly visitations as actual events or else as delusions or dreams.

But what if angels are real? What if they come in unexpected moments and in unsuspected ways to rouse the divine element within the human makeup? What if Kundalini itself is begotten of such angelic source, a mark of the divine claim upon us, a bond that cannot be broken? What if Kundalini is in fact another name for what some call angels? Both Kundalini and angels as we know them are of a higher frequency, and one wonders if thus they are simply different expressions of the same reality?

Perhaps unconditional love is just this: to be taken into the embrace of angels (Kundalini) and in that state to know what a divinized human can attain.

And now the final paradox emerges: What if the angelic being who seizes us in such love is in fact a version of ourselves, as we may once have been, in this realm or another? What if we are, all of us, turning into angels, as we reenact the glory from which we come?

When such as I cast out remorse
So great a sweetness flows into the breast
We must laugh and we must sing,
We are blest by everything,
Everything we look upon is blest.

—W. B. Yeats

RILKE AND ANGELS

Rainer Maria Rilke (1875–1926), one of the greatest poets of the modern era, was in love with angels. They inhabit his poetry, beckoning and calling at every turn. It is as if they were a secret presence, something sensed but never seen, suspected but not substanced. He longs for them eternally, yet he dreads their coming, their terrifying presence. And he asks, who among us could sustain such encounter?

He causes us to reflect that we, as humans, can bear only so much of divine reality. No one can encounter the full force of the sacred essence and live.

Here is an excerpt from Rilke's great series of poems called *The Duino Elegies* (Duino is the place where this brilliant sequence was written):

Who, if I cried, would hear me among the angelic
orders? And even if one of them suddenly
pressed me against his heart, I should fade in the strength of his
stronger existence. For Beauty's nothing
but beginning of Terror we're still just able to bear,
and why we adore it so is because it serenely
disdains to destroy us.

(from *The First Duino Elegy*, tr. Leishman and Spender)

WHAT IS THE SHEKHINAH?

I am reading an article about a renowned scholar who is currently translating the several volumes of the Kabbalah from Aramaic into English. The scholar explains that the word "Kabbalah" means receiving, being open to new insights about god or the nature of reality. And the primary book of the Kabbalah is the Zohar, which means radiance or splendor.

He then goes on to explain that god in this mystical system is equally male and female. The name of god as female is "Shekhinah" or the presence of god. We humans are charged to make god whole in our lives by bringing the two halves together. "We do that by ethical living."

He adds, "god is infinite energy." The Kabbalah has "insights that are important for any spiritual seeker."

His explanations left me with questions. Somehow, I had associated the Shekhinah with bliss itself, descent of supreme rapture, ecstasy even. In other words, I had assumed it was a manifestation of the energies of Kundalini, the one some call the goddess above all goddesses. If my assumption is true, this would explain why the study of this esoteric approach to the divine was always confined to a carefully chosen few, why the student was not allowed to begin his studies until he had reached the mature age of forty, why Kabbalists were viewed with suspicion as members of a group with questionable motives.

Where had I gotten such notions? I decided to look up the word shekhinah in some of the books by earlier feminist writers exploring the whole area of feminine spirituality.

Shekhinah was given various interpretations as the feminine principle. Many were the attributes commonly associated with the idea of female: kind, loving, compassionate, nurturing, gentle, motherly—the familiar list.

But nobody mentioned bliss. No one alluded to ecstasy. Energy, yes.

Ecstasy, no.

Somehow, these writers appeared to have missed a key element. If indeed "god" in female form is receptive, if the divine is energy, if woman is body-centered, if feeling is the realm of the female—how could bliss not be present?

In yogic philosophy, Shiva is likewise a dual god—shakti being his female half. And shakti is the term commonly used in Hindu to refer to the divine energy that literally enters the body of the devotee and bestows ineffable bliss as a sign of union.

In the course of my research, I came across an account of an early "spiritual initiation" of Marion Woodman, the renowned Jungian psychologist known especially for her work in dream interpretation.

When the (Episcopalian) bishop placed his hands on her head in her confirmation ceremony, a shock of energy raced through her body. "The light in my head was so brilliant that for an instant I couldn't see anything." Shaktipat? Kundalini? the Shekhinah?

However, Marion ultimately decided that she didn't want a priest standing between her and the experience of the sacred. In the privacy of her own living room, she "enters the unknown through her own body." She explains: "I stand with my arms outstretched or dance or lie flat on the floor and listen with my whole body. This is my connection to Sophia, to the Shekhinah."

I wonder how many of us do the same. We may give it another name, but it is the divine encounter, the holy embrace, piercing our very cells and molecules in ultimate love.

(Note: I do not mean to minimize in the least the role of compassion, of thoughtful action, or of ethical conduct in human affairs, but merely want to say there is also something more. God is more than an insight or an action. God is also experienced as a feeling, and to ignore that feeling is to cut god in half once more.)

THE SECRET TEACHINGS (BY GERALD MASSEY)

I have always been fascinated by anything that contained the words "secret" or "mystery" or "teachings." Even as a child, I fantasized hiding (or finding) secret treasures, things beyond price which the world knew nothing of.

So, today, when I received an announcement for a new edition of an early work by Gerald Massey (now deceased), I followed up by checking out the book's description on Amazon. In the course of my research, I came upon an amazing illustration from the back cover of the book and tried to copy it but was not successful. Here is the description of what the picture portrays:

[A photo that appears on] the back of the dust-jacket of The Secret Teachings is a scene engraved on a wall in the Temple of Luxor. It shows one of the greatest of the Egyptian pharaohs, Amenhotep III "the Magnificent," receiving the imposition of the Sa, or magnetic fluid, from the god Amun. "After having placed the peschent upon the head of the Pharaoh, who kneels before him, Amun proceeds to impose the Sa. The gods were not all equally charged with this magic fluid or life-energy. Some had more, others less, this they willingly gave to those who lacked it, and all could readily transmit it to mankind"—G. Maspero in *The Dawn of Civilization*

Could the "life-energy"—the "magnetic"—be Kundalini, and could the initiation by the god be an ancient enactment of what we today call Shaktipat? I suspect that it is. "Magnetic fluid" is an accurate description of what Kundalini feels like when it is flowing. And indeed, Kundalini is the "life-force." Kundalini has long been associated with secret rites and rituals, unusual powers, such as a Pharaoh might have possessed. And once one feels the awakened Kundalini, it often is as though one has been visited by a god or goddess.

In fact, some writers (such as William Irwin Thompson) have asserted that the erect cobra that the Pharaoh wears at the front of his or her head piece represents risen Kundalini (itself often depicted symbolically as a snake which rises).

In India, from ancient times, the fully risen Kundalini was symbolized as Shiva in union with Shakti (the female aspect of Shiva) at the crown. This union occurs when the "magnetic fluid" opens the crown chakra to allow the initiate to merge with the gods.

As I read further on this site, I ran across another quote from *The Secret Teachings* that caught my attention. It is quite different, yet also intriguing:

The following quotation from the Maitri Upanishad is one of the few attempts to describe this state of consciousness ("heavenly consciousness") or being and can serve as a rare example:

"Incomprehensible is the Supreme Self, unlimited, unborn, not to be reasoned about, unthinkable, He whose Self is space. At the dissolution of all, He alone remains awake. Thus from that space, He awakes this world which consists of thought only. By him alone is all this meditated on and in Him it is dissolved. He is that luminous form which gives heat in the yonder sun, the wonderful light on the smokeless fire, as also the fire which digests food.

"For thus is it said, 'He who is in the fire, and He who is here in the heart and He who is yonder in the sun—He is One. He who knows this goes to the Oneness of the One.' "

I was especially drawn to the statement that the world is made and re-made by the One, who creates the universe from thought itself. Science perpetually tries to discover how the world was made, but never finds the answer, because it is looking for a material origin. I happen to believe that consciousness preceded matter, and the latter resulted when that awareness chose to cast reality once more into material form.

The final sentence says, it seems, that god is in everything—the sun, the smokeless fire, and the digestive process itself. The first and last were indeed mysteries to the human (at least at that early time). But what is the "smokeless fire?" Could it be the radiant aura that surrounds objects when they are viewed in the light of astral plane? Or is it simply the fire that is produced from fuel that is totally combusted?

Of course, the above are all personal beliefs, but they are places I like to go to in thought when I am alone.

(Note: I am not endorsing this book—just thought it was interesting to pursue some of its ideas.)

LOVE AND FEAR

To transcend fear..., we must move somewhere else emotionally; we must move into love.

Happiness, anxiety, joy, resentment—we have many words for the many emotions we experience in our lifetimes. But deep down, at our cores, there are only two emotions: love and fear. All positive emotions come from love, all negative emotions from fear. From love flows happiness, contentment, peace, and joy. From fear comes anger, hate, anxiety and guilt.

—Elisabeth Kubler-Ross

Yes, what we yearn for is love—from others, from god, for self, for others, for god. And I think this is what Kundalini can in fact give to us. Even whe we do not have a close human partner, we know that we are in fact loved by an inexhaustible divine source, that which gives us life and sustains us and often visits in the form of the Beloved Within. This is what Kundalini in its highest form does—it takes away fear (our sense of inner loss, our neuroses that grow from such fear, our loneliness and despair) and gives us instead a realization of overwhelming acceptance and love from that reality which most matters—the overarching presence of which we ourselves are a part.

ENOUGH

I think it is enough,
at times,
to go without knowing
where the end is,
what the beginning—
so long ago.

Perhaps you have friends
who can whisper
such things
in your ear,
hear little bits of
messages
in the laughter of children.

But mostly we just proceed ahead,
not remembering
how it all started,
where it is leading,
not sure
if we are the waiting animal
or the animal's passing
shadow
in the grass.

BHAKTI (DEVOTION)

Devotion attracts Him
Devotion reveals him;
the Lord is influenced by devotion.
Nothing is more powerful than bhakti.

—from the *Mathara-Sruti* (ancient Hindu text)

What is devotion? It is when we feel divine essence enter our bodies and know that we and it are One. It is the time when we go into that state of being which enables us to feel that which otherwise is hidden from us. It occurs when we know that we have entered sacred presence, and our heart gives thanks, and asks nothing more than to enjoy this moment of precious connection.

Devotion is not praying for "something" that is desired. It is entering into a condition of union with that which is, when we know that nothing more is needed.

IS KUNDALINI CATCHING?

Someone has asked whether or not Kundalini is "catching." And indeed it is. Partners sometimes "catch" Kundalini from one another. You can "pick up vibes" from friends or strangers, and even from what you read on your computer (e-mail and entries on the internet) or in books. In part, I think much of this depends on how your own energies are functioning—it is especially easy to detect such vibrations from others at the beginning of your Kundalini process, when your own system may be virtually wide open. Even later, your sensitivity may vary from time to time—when you sense your energies strong within, you are more likely to be aware of emanations from outside sources.

The strength of your energies will likely vary from day to day, and there is no predicting when they will be intense, when less so. Earlier this month, I described exquisite energies flowing within, but a few days later, this intensity abated. Today my practice was essentially just simple stretching and movement.

I always begin "meditation" (standing with gentle moves, sensing the energetic flows within) with no expectations. On some days, I am "surprised by joy," and on others it is more like plain exercise (though even then, I think of it as connection through sacred movement).

REMEMBERING PAST LIVES

Here is a vision I experienced today in my morning meditation.

In San Francisco (where I recently visited) I had picked up two very inexpensive CDs from a Tibet shop that was going out of business. One of these was entitled "Tibet's Garden" from Nature Harmonics. I got the impression from the jacket that this would be a recording of nature sounds in Tibet, and frankly, I was a little bit disappointed, since I was longing for music.

Sure enough the first sound was that of roaring wind, with a soft undertone of horns beneath it. My first reaction was that this was not a very good recording—the sound was abrasive and the musical notes too faint to hear clearly.

As I listened, the sound of the wind unleashed made me think of how such sounds must have been common around the monasteries poised on the edge of steep cliffs in Tibet, and I almost shivered to think of how cold these temples must have been.

And then, I seemed to perceive a small procession coming from the monastery, with monks bearing a corpse on a litter. I assumed it was being taken away for a "sky burial," the practice in which ancient Tibetans carried the corpse to a remote spot where designated monks dismembered it and left the remains for the vultures to dispose of. I did not know for sure the identity of the corpse, but I felt strongly that it was me (but I was not disturbed at all by this idea—after death the body has no more purpose in this world and should be destroyed in any way that is appropriate).

And then another image came up. This time I knew it was me—I was a young boy, about fourteen years old, who had just arrived at a monastery hoping to be given shelter and to be trained as a monk. He (I) was very frightened, for he had never been anywhere at all before, outside the place where he lived (a horse ranch in Tibet), and everything here was new and strange. He was overwhelmed by the thought of what lay ahead, and most of all, afraid he would not be accepted or be able to do things in the proper way. Above all, he wanted to please, to follow correct procedures, and for now he was extremely anxious about his new life among these august elders.

Next day, he was given a bath, had his head shaved, and received a robe. His old clothes were burned.

At first, the young man was not allowed to sleep inside the monastery. He was sent to the stables to sleep with the animals. This did not bother him, for that was where he usually slept.

A few days later, after he was more presentable, he was taken into the presence of the Head Abbott, who questioned him about his background and reasons for coming:

Can you write?

I can write my name.

Do you know your numbers?

I can write to 20.

Can you read?

I can recognize a few Sanskrit letters.

The Abbott then told him he could stay and become a monk.

It was an extremely powerful experience and, although I am not a crier, I began to sob with the enormity of the revelation. It was as though a veil had been lifted and I, at last, was permitted to know (experience) who I was in a former life.

It was as if I had indeed entered his body, taken on his emotions, and in fact, I realized that this emotional and energetic body was my own. It felt totally familiar because we were one and the same and his was the subtle body I had carried with me into this life, including an innate shyness and a profound desire to please.

I might add that I immediately loved him, and realized he was most tender and sweet in his own right. I felt toward him the way any one of us might (in this life) feel about ourselves when we had been young and vulnerable.

Actually, I have had somewhat similar glimpses of myself as a monk a few times before. Once when I was getting a massage, I "nodded off" and seemed to be a monk who was drifting in and out of consciousness as he lay dying. All the while, he was surrounded by other monks chanting over him. This was in no way frightening, but just the opposite—it was a very easy and supported death.

Another time I got a glimpse of "myself" as the Abbott of a monastery (again, in Tibet). I took one look at this rather good looking and extremely poised person and thought, "This fellow is no ascetic, that's for sure."

And at another time, I saw myself as a rather pudgy monk who helped in the kitchen. He was a little bit disheveled and needed to comb his hair, but he was happy in his humble life.

These latter images were merely glimpses, but the vision of this morning was a full blown and totally convincing recovery of a buried memory. I felt it revealed a blessing that had been granted, and knew that this moment of entry into a new life led directly to where (and who) I am now.

Later, I went over to a nearby restaurant for breakfast, and carried with me a volume of poems by Kabir (translated by Tagore) because I wanted to maintain the special state of deep consciousness I was in. At the restaurant, I opened to a previously bookmarked (but forgotten) page and read these lines:

> *I became suddenly revealed in Benares,*
> *and Ramananda illumined me;*
> *I brought with me the thirst for the Infinite*

and I have come for the meeting with Him.
In simplicity I will unite with the Simple One;
my love will surge up.

Yeats says that the final moment of revelation comes "when naked to naked goes," when our ego attachments and identity presumptions are surrendered and we encounter ultimate reality (or as much of it as we are prepared to bear).

Indeed, many of us know the "thirst for the Infinite" as a major force that shapes our lives. As we in time discover our "past selves," the source of our longing may be revealed.

MORE ON PAST LIFE RECALL

Yesterday, I virtually vibrated in bliss all day, from the effects of the morning's experience of recollection. Today I expected merely to do a few stretches and continue with other activities, but then I decided to play yesterday's CD to see what might arise in consciousness. But almost immediately, my inner spirit began to protest: "I don't want to die that death again." So I moved silently, and the energies were again another experience like light moving over and through the body with very subtle movement. And at that point I seemed to remember more of yesterday's tale, although this time it was not as obvious as to whether this was an actual memory or my own imagination supplying the details. This is what came up:

I had arrived at the monastery before dawn—the monks were performing their morning rituals, so I was kept waiting in the anteroom. I was terrified. I had never been anywhere at all beyond my most recent home on the horse farm. Then, since I had walked a long distance and was wearing mud-caked clothes, I was sent to sleep with the animals, lest I had brought along some unwelcome travelers (fleas or lice). Of course, this was not at all disturbing to me, since it was where I usually slept. Later I was allowed to take a bath and given a fresh robe to wear. My head was shaved and my old clothes were burned. I was fed and then allowed to rest again (I was exhausted, for I had walked many miles to the monastery and had not had anything to eat). For three days, I was permitted to witness the chanting ceremonies of the sangha, but of course could not participate in the rituals.

Then I was sent for the interview with the Abbott of the monastery. He was a serious but not unkind man in his fifties. I was quite tense and frightened during the interview. He asked what kind of work I did before, and I explained that I had served a master who had me help with caring for the many horses on this horse ranch, milking the goats, and similar tasks. I said that I had come because an inner voice had urged me to find this monastery and live there.

Then he asked if there had been some kind of trouble at home, and I had to confess that there had been. My first master had been kind to me—he gave me food to eat, clothes to wear, and a place to sleep. But he had died and his cousin, who took over, was quite harsh. He did not beat me, but he did others in his service, and I was very troubled by this. A traveling lama had once come through, performed puja and described the monastery as a wonderful place, so I had decided to seek it out and become a monk.

The Abbott seemed satisfied and sent me to the kitchen so I could be assigned my duties. I think my original assignment was emptying and cleaning the slop buckets from the various rooms. I was grateful to have this job and determined to do it as best I could.

In this morning's meditation I received a few more brief glimpses of the lifetime that had emerged two days ago. First, I had the sense of baskets being carried filled with—what? flowers? fruit? No, neither of these. Finally, it came. It was yak dung, used for fuel in the monastery. It had been my job to carry buckets and buckets of these up the steep incline to the temple. I did not mind this humble assignment. Rather I was thrilled and kept repeating to myself in delight, "I have a job! I have a job!"

Indeed, what I recalled most vividly from this memory were the deep emotions I experienced—the terror of the arrival, the joy of my assignment.

Then there was a flash to another time, another "me," now much more mature and evolved, someone who had a position of responsibility in the *sangha*. I wondered how many times he had bowed or made obeisance to the Buddha in the main hall and somehow this act was related to my present sense of deep reverence for and connection with the Buddha in my thangka.

My energies, so pronounced early on, had now diminished, and were now like delicate streams of light playing here and there over the body. Once more, the initial surge after the full moon was the strongest, but these diminished day by day after the onset. We'll see what happens in the future.

This morning, after these musings, I played part of a CD that contained chanting to a background of horns, drums, and cymbals. I think I was not a musician in that lifetime, but I had in fact at some point learned to be a dancer, so now, I even performed a few heavy turns on my own rug. Somehow I can't resist movement, once those wild horns begin to sound along with that strange but fascinating clang and clamor of cymbal and drums.

One wonders what will come next as we go forward into this time of radical change on all levels. I think we will have to surrender many of our assumptions and expectations as to what is possible, how our universe operates, and who we are as we are being thrust up to new levels of awareness. Part of the challenge will be to stay open to the unfamiliar inner shifts while maintaining as much balance as possible—it is indeed as if we are walking a tightrope over a chasm, but fortunately we have guidance to protect and lead us as we advance (metaphorically) together. Indeed, this is the time we have waited for, the moment of all moments in human history.

See thou everything
As thine own dwelling place:
the mist of pleasure and pain
can never spread there.
There Brahma is revealed
day and night: there light
is His garment,
light is His seat,
light rests on thine head.
Kabir says, "The Master,
who is true,
He is all light."

—from "Songs of Kabir" (tr. Tagore)

Recently I spent two weeks in the Bay Area. I had a wonderful time, visiting with close friends, traveling up to Big Sur on a perfect sunny day, and going to the incredible Monterey aquarium, one of the most highly rated in the country. But later I reflected that my good time had not included any "mystical moments," but rather was composed of the best of "ordinary consciousness." And, delightful as these were, none compared with the exquisite quality of the experience I encountered (intense bliss) on my return home. Perhaps I might say that the Beloved was waiting in my living room and our reunion was sweet.

What would it be like to live perpetually in a Buddha field, such as that created in an ancient monastery, when human consciousness of the higher reality was constantly reinforced by reminders of the transcendent? We can study history, gaze on early day paintings and relics, and listen to CDs, but we, as products of a different culture and time, can never fully enter into the state of awareness and feeling that marked each moment of those distant lives. They were, I think, shaped in a different mold, and our attempts to recapture those lost states of being can offer only minuscule tastes of such existence.

(from *Unmasking the Rose: A Record of a Kundalini Initiation*)

NICOLE GRACE AND ENLIGHTENMENT

I have been reading an interview with author Nicole Grace, who has recently published a book called *Bodhisattva: How to Be Free*. Nicole is a former organizational consultant who experienced a sudden, unexpected, and very dramatic awakening (we would call it Kundalini Awakening, though she does not use this term) and subsequently became a Buddhist monk, spiritual teacher, and writer on the topic of being a Bodhisattva.

For those who may not know, a Bodhisattva is one who foregoes enlightenment in this lifetime in order to help others attain this state. In earlier times, enlightenment was especially prized because it allowed one to enter nirvana and thus escape continuing rebirths into the human state, with its attendant sufferings and sorrows. Today we think of the Bodhisattva as someone who shows great compassion for others and who dedicates his/her life to alleviating the sufferings of this world.

Nicole's awakening occurred when she, as an adult, was simply listening to music. Suddenly, her crown opened, and "the light of the universe just poured in like a fire hose pointed down." Light (in both a metaphorical and literal sense) is often associated with spiritual awakening and with Kundalini. When it arrives in this fashion, it can in fact be quite disconcerting. I met one woman who said that when light visited her in this way, she was never really sure where to step, for everything, including the floor and her feet, seemed to be made of pure light.

Nicole is quite frank about her experience. She feels that it was not full enlightenment as such, but rather a "glimpse" or "taste" of enlightenment. She makes the important point that there are in fact "levels of enlightenment" and that just because one has had an initial experience, one may not remain permanently in this state at all, but rather undergo intermittent moments of similarly expanded consciousness.

I resonated deeply with many of Nicole's descriptions and observations. She describes her path as Tantric Buddhist mysticism, and says "...it's essentially the pathway to enlightenment through direct experience of the Divine, without the formal organized structures of the Buddhist religion." She explains that Tantra has mistakenly become associated specifically with sexual activities through misunderstanding. "Tantra" means "weaving" and includes "mysticism from every possible corner: Hinduism, Christian mysticism, Kabbalah, anything that works."

Oddly, though she advocates following the "direct path" to the divine, she herself quickly located a teacher to lead her through her transformational process. I am not sure how she reconciles this apparent contradiction.

Although she offers workshops and presentations to many thousands of listeners, she does not allow her picture to be posted on the internet or on her book cover, for fear of being turned into a guru (cult) figure. She also refuses to divulge the name of her teacher, considering this to be too private for public revelation.

Note: Nicole's chosen spiritual name is Kundalini. I wonder if she knows how many today are undergoing deep and sudden transformation through Kundalini awakening and thus would be (according to her view) in danger of being turned into cult figures.

We are going through this process together on a massive scale and thus we must be teachers to one another.

KUNDALINI, ENLIGHTENMENT, AND THE NEAR-DEATH EXPERIENCE

Tonight I watched a TV program on the Biography channel, focusing on the Near-Death Experience. Three NDE survivors told their stories—one was Barbara Harris Whitfield, a friend whom I have met through Kundalini activities. As many may know, a Near-Death Experience is considered to be much like a Kundalini awakening, and the groups follow parallel paths in many ways.

I will not relate the individual stories here, other than to say that the three persons who described their experiences all left their bodies, and were judged clinically dead for many minutes, one for almost an hour. All told of the bliss and serenity they felt as they watched the medical teams labor below to resuscitate them, and of their reluctance to return to their physical bodies with its attendant pain and challenges.

Each one told of feeling as though they were enveloped in a vast field of love while they were no longer connected with their physical beings. They felt that this—their spirit body—was their real identity. When they "returned" (and recovered) they brought with them a new realization of the true values of their own lives. As Barbara put it, they knew that the truth lay "inside" (the life of the spirit) rather than "outside" (the world of "things" and mundane activities). For each one, love became the supreme focus of their lives, and loving and receiving love the most important aspect of living.

It occurred to me after I watched this program, that what they learned is also the lesson of Enlightenment itself. The lesson is that reality (truth) in fact is a great field of energy whose tone and texture is love itself. To be enlightened in the ancient sense is to learn that one is merely a part of this great sea of love energy, and that loving others is the supreme reflection of this truth.

So—we do not have to sit in a cave and bring the energies up through the Sushumna in order to reach Enlightenment (though this is one method, for it culminates in union with divine love). Nor must we undergo a

Near-Death Experience to reach this state. There is another way and it is open to each of us every minute of our lives. It has nothing to do with religion or religious institutions as such. We need only to practice love, to offer and receive love, and know that we are all connected through love.

MORE ON KUNDALINI AND NEAR-DEATH EXPERIENCES

Last night I attended a fascinating panel by persons who had gone through a Near-death Experience. Once more, I was struck by the resemblance between NDEs and Kundalini awakening. Here are some of their common features (often noted by other writers as well):

1. Each is a life-changing event. It is what Katherine Anne Porter called (in another context) "the moment that changes everything." Once such profound encounters occur, one is changed forever and there is no going back to the earlier stage.

2. Both result in states of overwhelming love. Those who travel to "the other side" are so enraptured by their new sense of indescribable bliss that they feel that they are embraced by the vast and loving forces of the universe, even god itself. Likewise, Kundalini, when it is in proper alignment, may result in absolute ecstasy, akin to that of St. Teresa of Avila or St. John of the Cross. This condition of utter bliss is not a thought but a somatic experience at the cellular level.

3. Both find in this new state that feelings of depression or self-rejection simply disappear, for surely one cannot be sad in the face of such overwhelming love. Atheists become believers, doubters are convinced. The "divine" is real and courses through the body as the Beloved Within.

4. Both have great difficulty in "returning" to the world where materialistic values and petty concerns are the norm. They are now "walking in the two worlds," for they have been granted a vision of a reality that others do not know exists.

5. Both are often reluctant to share this mysterious and intimate adventure with others, for it seems like a betrayal of that which is profoundly sacred. Ultimately, they may come forth and speak, as a gift to the world to help understand this still unfamiliar experience.

6. Both now often have a sense of mission or purpose, and seek a means

of "giving back" the gift in whatever way is best suited to their capacities. They may go into healing professions, or turn to artistic expressions, or writing. Service, rather than personal gain, is now their motivating factor.

7. Both experience great love for and a sense of oneness with all others. They literally feel "I am you" and if I look in the mirror, it might be your face that I see. The world itself may appear in radiant beauty, transformed into a garden of mystic delight. Everything, even the trash in the street, may be luminous. They may know at the deepest levels that everything and every being in the universe is connected as part of the one great whole, as part of the single fabric of the cosmos with love at the center of all.

8. They may be quite lonely in their journey, for others may be disbelieving or openly disapproving when they attempt to describe their encounters. Family and friends may think they are mentally disturbed and need psychological help. Mates may feel betrayed and see this new element as a disrupting element in their relationship. Indeed, they may have no one to confide in, no one to support them as they struggle to integrate this new dimension of awareness into their lives.

8. Both NDEers and Kundalini awakened ones may now be filled with the deep realization that each of us is a "fiction," a story that we ourselves have created, for we do not exist except as tiny particle in the great glory of the divine source.

9. Each experience is unique to the person. Each one undergoes a pattern of responses relevant to their particular nature and life experiences. Yet there are common threads among all of these.

10. Universal awareness of both the NDE and Kundalini processes is becoming more widespread, in part because of media access and also because (I think) more such events are actually happening as the field expands, especially those involving spontaneous Kundalini awakenings.

11. Both phenomena are (I believe) parts of the ongoing process of evolution of consciousness now going on worldwide. Both propel us forward as humanity transforms into a new kind of being, indeed perhaps a new species.

12. One of the dominant features of the NDE is the immersion into a sea of love at the other side. Kundalini itself often produces a similar feeling of ecstatic joy. Some authorities state that at the moment of death, the Kundalini energies are released and thus one may exit in a state of pure rapture. Thus Kundalini is in fact an integral part of the death process itself.

The folks on the panel were each one a loving being, transformed into a messenger of the heart to help the planet move forward in our process of universal awakening to a new reality.

ON KUNDALINI AND THE SACRED

Today, with the recent increase in Kundalini phenomena, many investigations are attempting to reduce the experience to a "nothing but" event: to a measurable psycho-physiological play of the nervous system; to a series of symptoms ranging from the bizarre to the psychotic; to a singular component of a larger delusional syndrome.

Kundalini may include aspects of any or all of the above. It may bring with it curious readjustments of the psyche as well as the bio-network; it may trigger a passing symptomology both unfamiliar and disturbing; it may awaken deep memory, buried racial and archetypal themes. But Kundalini is far more than an electromagnetic impulse; it is not merely another pathology of mind or body; it is based on far other than delusion. Kundalini is well documented as part of the practice of seekers in ancient times. Today, Kundalini is one of the last remaining instruments we as humans possess for entry into the world of the sacred. It is the unimaginably powerful agent for putting us—we, the intellectually sophisticated ones of the contemporary world—in touch with those lost realms in which many of our ancestors dwelt in intimate relation with an unseen but powerful reality.

Kundalini is often compared to a snake which bites as it rises—and indeed it cuts through—it conveys us quickly into the heart of the "self-validating experience." It is also often depicted as a goddess, indeed sometimes it is termed "the goddess above all other goddesses." Kundalini is the energy behind the image, the vibrational emanation empowering the symbol. It is the divine in its purest, most naked form. On the human level it is a feeling, not an assertion, and thus because it is experienced with such fullness and finality at the very core of being, we feel that it needs no confirmation through intellectual affirmation or mental acknowledgment. This is not to say we do not ask, "What is this mysterious power?" nor seek to discover the secrets of its origin and its mode of operation. But—beyond these—the discernible physiological facts, the electromagnetic observations—emerges an entire body of evidence, non-measurable, unweighted, yet of infinite persuasiveness and conviction.

Like the aesthetic response, it carries a convincingness beyond the explainable. Like the mystic moment, it rests within the assurance of its own ineffable reality.

What, then, is Kundalini? Most immediately, it is an experience of the body/spirit which yields bliss not accessible to the ordinary senses. And this moment of transcendent rapture carries with it deep conviction of union with that which exists beyond the mere self. It confirms, however transitory, that we, as conscious beings, are part and parcel of a larger reality whose outlines and composition we can but barely guess. For that time, words, pronouncements, the idle chatter within, are suspended— we are, as the cliché would have it—at one with the infinite. We have heard these words too many times to accept them without challenge. Yet, simple and shopworn as they are, they tell us of our perennial yearning to connect—to join—to locate and consciously merge with our own original source, which we may not accurately name but whose presence stirs in us perpetually.

Kundalini opens the gates to sacred space. One who seeks access to these precincts in order merely to probe or gauge or measure will miss its identifying features entirely. He might as well cut open the heart to locate the seat of the soul, or explore the essence of matter merely by reducing a substance into finer and finer particles. This one will discover no spirit guide, no sacred groves. Like the investigator who seeks to explore with a lantern the nature of darkness, he will drive before him the evidence he seeks. For him the charms will fail, the alchemy falter. He lacks the language of this foreign territory, and hence will never unlock its meaning or capture its truth.

(from *Unmasking the Rose*)

STAYING IN OUR COMFORT ZONE

Recently, I watched a television interview with Janet, a psychic/healer. Many of her comments struck a resonant chord with me, such as her statement that we often choose to set limits to how far we are willing to go in the area of "expanded consciousness" in order to protect ourselves.

This can be a very good thing. If we go too far into the "unknown," we may induce fear and even panic if we get in over our heads. On the other hand, if we close down too tightly, we will fail to develop our own inner capacities. I like the idea of going as far as feels right and comfortable. If it doesn't feel right, and in particular if it seems too "scary," it is probably best to back off and leave that particular avenue alone.

Your gut and your heart will tell you how much is right for you.

However, we should also add that once Kundalini starts, it must continue until it is finished. There is no reason to "fear," since what is happening is an internal process unique to you, and your "inner guide" will take you home if you will relax and allow it to do its work (and this may take a long time and be challenging for a while).

The psychic also mentioned that true awakening is a gift, and no amount of practice and devotion can induce it if the timing is not right. No one knows why some receive the gift, and others—it is grace itself that determines the outcome—but many more are being "brought into the fold" at this critical juncture in our lives.

Janet also added that we are each here to carry some part of the vibrational spectrum governing earth's purpose. Thus each of us has a special role to play, and those in touch with the subtle realms have—in my mind—a particular responsibility not only to "carry the vibration" but to help others advance on their own spiritual paths.

THE RAPTURE OF MUSIC

A few weeks ago, I visited Mendocino, a town located north of San Francisco.

As I walked along the trail above the cliffs on which the city is perched, I heard music coming from a large tent above. I went up to investigate, and found the Mendocino summer orchestra rehearsing for the night's performance of Mendelssohn's Piano Concerto # 2.

First I took a modest seat near the back of the auditorium. Then I slipped down about midway. (The tent was almost empty of listeners.) Finally, I went forward as far as I could go, so that I was all but under the piano.

And there she was, an incredible pianist I had never heard of, playing with great energy and flair, each stroke a dynamic gesture that aroused impulses of exquisite bliss within my body. Each pore seemed to open, and I felt as though I was literally trying to leave my body in ecstatic levitation. It was totally rapturous, totally ravishing, touching every single cell and membrane.

Afterwards, I approached her and told her she had truly opened my chakras. "Me too," she said, "at least on a good day."

Here is the poem I wrote:

THE REHEARSAL

'An ornament of the eternal,'
that poet said.

As, indeed, that pianist there

in the huge tent billowing on the cliff
overlooking the sea,
performing with nothing
but her fingers and notes
and keys laid out over a huge black box,
and the orchestra swelling
against her in the background,
and what that did to
our straining bodies,
every pore illumined by bliss,
our hearts speeding
as if we were being
lifted up,
ascension of levitation,
even our hands opening
to a dense pleasure,
shameless intensity,
hopeless vibration of rapture,
the kingdom discovered at last.

THE CRYSTAL BED, ENLIGHTENMENT

A few years ago, I began the New Year in San Francisco, visiting with friends, going to museums and rediscovering the incredible cuisine of that city. All my time was delightful, but perhaps the highlight was my experience on the Crystal Bed. This took place in a recently established healing center there, one with lovely vibrations and lovely young people operating it. It was the sort of place you would be happy to come to just to sit quietly and meditate if nothing else.

The Crystal Bed is the creation of John of god, the famous healer who lives in Brazil. Many people make the long journey to visit him, and some experience magical healings, while others report no real changes. Since he charges nothing for his services, he obviously is not attempting to grow rich from his gifts.

The Crystal Bed, which at first existed only in his healing center, now is available in this country in various venues. The bed itself is a simple massage table with a series of clear crystals suspended over it, each located above a certain chakra. Lights of various colors shine through the crystals, each corresponding to the color of the chakra it illuminates.

My session was only 20 minutes, since I wanted merely to taste the experience and did not have time to stay longer.

When I lay down (with my eyes blindfolded to protect from the lights) I immediately saw (within) a clear image of a woman's face, someone I did not recognize. Who is this person? I wondered, since she resembled no one I knew. She was young—maybe 35 or so, with jet black hair drawn back from her slim oval face. I felt she was of some specific ethnicity, and thought she most suggested a native American or someone of Latina heritage. Then I slipped into a slightly different state of consciousness.

I did not feel anything similar to Kundalini energies. Rather, I felt deep relaxation coming over me, with tension and release occurring in the various chakras, from the root up. After what seemed to be a long time, the session was over.

Afterward, I shared my inner vision with Rubi and Archimedes, the delightful young operators of the center. Without saying anything, Archimedes stepped across the room and returned with a small statuette of a winged Native American Angel, and I realized that this was indeed the face I had seen. He told me that she was often present in the center, and clearly she helped with the healing process offered there.

Then Rubi, who had sat nearby to "hold the field" during my session, said that she had also seen an inner image, this at the very end of my time on the table. As the session was closing, she saw a dervish whirling upward from my crown, spiraling toward heaven. I told her that I had recently made friends with several Sufis, and so the image seemed relevant.

Then, when I was riding a city bus a few days later, I saw a woman sitting across from me who looked identical to my inner vision. She even had her hair parted in the middle, like the woman in my mind. So it was as though I had met the "angel" in the flesh, now incarnated as an actual person.

As for Enlightenment, I did not become enlightened in San Francisco, though I did go to a moving exhibit of Thai and Burmese art at the Asian Art Museum. Again, I felt no special energies, but loved the sense of quiet emanating from the many Buddhas on display. The sculpture that most captivated me was one of Buddha's chief disciples, resting at his feet and gazing upward in loving adoration. He somehow reminded me of many Asian monks I have seen, small androgynous males quietly loving and gentle.

Then, this morning, I was perusing a website of a spiritual teacher who asserts that if only 5% of the population became enlightened, that would effect the sudden transformation of the entire world. He also stated that the age of gurus was past, and that we must all now share with one another as we advance together into the new stage of humanity. I think he is right. And he repeated the lesson we are hearing again and again from many quarters—we are all one, part of one creation, yoked in common purpose.

So as this and all future new years proceed, let us all love and bless one another, and together create our own crystal field of enlightenment as we prepare for the change that is even now occurring worldwide. This is indeed why we came.

part 4

FURTHER REFLECTIONS

ON THE LONGING FOR A PERFECT BODY

All of us yearn for a perfect body—a vessel total and complete on all the levels, physical, mental, emotional, and energetic/spiritual. But in truth no one (at least no one that I know of) ever attains this ideal. Even after we are visited by the divine energies, even when we have been opened to extreme ecstasy as a gift of grace, there remain flaws, impediments of various kinds. Beginning meditators sometimes suppose they will be instantly plunged into states of total serenity and calm, only to discover that all their hidden issues surface during these periods of quiet. Kundalini can bring extreme bliss, but it can also turn a spotlight on any unresolved psychological or physical problems.

So our lives remain forever a series of challenges, a constantly shifting flow of pleasures interwoven with pain. Shadow invariably accompanies sun. Descent follows arrival at the apex. Full enlightenment (if that implies absolute perfection of being) is not available on this earth. Nonetheless, we constantly continue our search for bliss, and inevitably encounter moments of transcendence followed by the downward swing.

It is the glimpses, the brief tastes of nirvana (sometimes very rich), which lure us forward, giving us reassurance that our journey is not in vain, that the reward we seek is waiting somewhere up ahead and ultimately attainable. In such times as our own, when the world is wracked by chaos, when human suffering of all kinds is so prevalent, we need this comfort, this sudden visitation of the unseen even in the midst of turmoil. Some turn to human love, some continue to seek the divine embrace. But always, whatever the path, there will be times of pain and suffering as well as the moments of exaltation.

Blake said, "Without contraries is no progression." By moving through the contraries, we together approach planetary initiation, Teilhard de Chardin's "Omega Point," the place where divine and human meet in final union.

PRE-BIRTH AGREEMENTS

Let us say that somewhere, in a time not known, in a place not named, "you" (in whatever guise you then existed in that other realm) volunteered for a cosmic project. You did not know the full nature of that project (other than that it was profoundly benevolent toward the universe), nor did you learn your exact role, nor how the full scenario would play out.

You agreed to enter the earth-field and to undergo birth as an "earth-being," through the common biological processes of that sphere. You were informed that once you were "conceived" (made ready) your memory bank would be scrubbed, and that you would no longer recall your origins nor your previous nature nor even the conditions under which you came. You would be "shrunk" in the process, reduced from your state as a freely roving spirit with near limitless abilities and knowledge, to a small, seriously restricted being, subject to all the challenges and difficulties of the human plane. Pain and agony and frustration would be part of your daily lot, along with all the rest of humanity struggling to survive in difficult circumstances.

Your task would be to discover and serve, as best you could, that central purpose for which you came. You would at some point be profoundly "awakened" to your inherent nature and given a glimpse of your appointed task, but even then you would not be privy to the overall design of this program nor to the designers and overseers. To a great extent, you would rely on faith itself that you were involved in a worthy scheme, one created to benefit humankind in crisis, and thus the cosmos itself.

Who, then, do you serve? How do you fulfill your "assignment"? How can you avoid the many "traps" which lie in wait, such as ego-inflation, the distractions of the myriad "trivial pursuits" which infest the modern scene? Must you forever struggle alone to fulfill your intention? How will you discover what you are supposed to do?

I think many of us share such intimations of serving an underlying larger purpose, a sense of connection with something unknown but of prime importance. Perhaps our feeling could be described simply as a general inclination toward good. Perhaps such intuitions stem from the soul's prior existence as an inhabitant of invisible celestial realms, the sphere of spirits who descend in order to serve in humility and compassion. (Many early writers have spoken of the pre-existence of the soul, including Plato and Wordsworth, who said that we came to earth "trailing clouds of glory.")

What can we say, other than together we struggle toward light? In the midst of world trauma and personal challenge, we open to transformation, allowing the renewed self to become the impetus for worldwide metamorphosis. One by one, we move into the unknown to allow the new humanity to be born.

Our souls enter holy union with the unseen divine, and thus we honor the "prenuptial agreements" which we know are our own.

Kundalini is one means by which the self is awakened to its own true nature and purpose. For this reason, I think that those who have experienced this process of semi-enlightenment bear a special responsibility to answer the world's cry for help at this time of extreme crisis. We are in a special category, for we know the fullness of love and the inherent joy of that invisible reality. Thus, even in the midst of what sometimes seems like universal catastrophe and woe, we can find grounds for affirmation, and discover reasons for hope. It is indeed as though god (the goddess) holds our hand as we walk through fields of fire.

KUNDALINI, ECSTASY, WISDOM, COMPASSION

Kundalini at its finest implies ecstatic joy, the overflowing into the body (or from the body) of a kind of divine rapture, a sense of deep and wondrous connection with the ultimate source.

But what, we may ask, does such intimate personal experience have to do with today's world, which is dominated by war and widespread human suffering? What right do any of us have to indulge in such subjective pleasures when the world so desperately needs all of us to attend to its critical needs, dress its wounds, solve its problems?

My answer is simple: even in the time of war, the sap continues to rise in the trees, the flowers bloom, and the animals cavort in the fields and bear their young. Nature does not cease because of human conflict and the grief it inflicts on its victims. When we "celebrate" love, through dancing, or singing, or simply feeling the flow of the inner currents, we affirm life itself, and thereby make ourselves more fit to be participants on the stage of the human struggles.

We do not cease to think because we allow ourselves to experience joy. We need not feel guilt because the heart of love throbs in our veins. Indeed, this is our challenge—to reconcile two seemingly disparate modes, the path of feeling which allows us to experience fully the bliss which is ours by divine right, and the path of thoughtfulness, which anchors us in the world about us. The mind itself is an important aspect of our being. We do not reject awareness of the world's chaotic affairs simply because we experience a few moments of private communion with "god" in our daily practice.

The call to wisdom demands that we do not retreat totally into the realm of subjective bliss (though at times such withdrawal seems quite attractive). We think and learn and grow, and only by the long labor of years of reflection and dedication can we claim to a modicum of "wisdom," that evanescent but essential ingredient so necessary to full development.

As for compassion, this is doubtless the most important of all human attributes, the epitome of all human virtue. Without compassion, bliss can easily become callous self-indulgence, and wisdom the arena for mere accumulation of "knowledge." Compassion for one another, concern for the welfare of the whole, not just the special chosen group, is the key for the world's salvation. Only when we cease to think in terms of "us" and "them," "ours" and "theirs," can we hope to create a world dedicated to the full development of the human, body and soul.

Kundalini bliss does not rule out wisdom nor preclude compassion. All are essential components of our total identity, our completion as children of the spirit as well as the flesh.

TWO KINDS OF INTELLIGENCE

There are two kinds of intelligence.
—Rumi

One is the sort
we acquire in school,
where we memorize,
dissect, discard
what our feelings tell us
about the real direction
our hearts wish to go.

Thus we develop skills
that command
a high price
in the market.
We marry our computers,
or learn to take the stuff
of this world apart,
ever finding new skills
to add to an already existing
array of proficiencies.

We thus are certain
that we know what we know,
and never have to think
about other possibilities,
sovereigns of our chosen
kingdoms.

We often become famous,
win prizes,
acclaimed for our discoveries
that make us ever more
marketable.

The other kind of knowledge
opens us to the secrets of
plants and paintings.
We marry certain trees
and betroth ourselves to flowers.
Evening clouds
take us aback
with their shifting
array of colors,
purple and subtle orange.
It envelops us
in a kind of awe at concerts,
where we allow ourselves
to be ravished
by sound, frequencies arriving
in nuanced order
to echo deep within.

This kind of knowing
commands love,
a caring for those
who cross our path,
a way of connecting with
others, even those
we have never seen.

This way is not marketable.

It constantly turns the base metal
of our lives into gold.

WHY SOME OF US ARE DIFFERENT

Many of us feel that somehow we have never "fit in." It is as if we actually originate from some other realm, some place of origin different from the "others." Wordsworth said of himself (when he was young) that he was "not of this time, not of this place," and he also asserted that we came into this world "trailing clouds of glory" from an unknown source.

I have often discussed this mystery with friends. Why do some seem to stumble blindly (or perhaps easily) through their lives, accepting the dictums of society, conforming freely to the given norms and expectations, apparently happy in their paths, while others are never really comfortable in their efforts to "fit in," often sensing that they are "different" in ways they can't quite describe.

And, furthermore, why is it that some seem to be more "open," "awake," in tune with invisible forces that others remain oblivious to? The former are often the real visionaries, the psychics, the mystics, the shamanic healers, those who sense the energies of what surrounds them, and, certainly, those who have undergone the mysterious process of Kundalini awakening. (Anyone who experiences such awakening at a deep level knows how extremely difficult it is to share this key event with others—often family, friends, doctors and therapists simply cannot comprehend this experience and may interpret it as a sign of mental imbalance or worse.)

At times, it seems as though there are two different races or strains among the group we name "the human species." Why are some more aware, more sensitive, more in touch with unseen realms?

Recently, I considered the theory that space travelers from other planets did indeed visit earth at some point in ancient history, and implant a new set of genes in what became the human race. Perhaps some of us now have more of those genes "turned on" in our systems, while others do not. Everyone carries this potential within, but some already are living this awakened state.

Tonight, watching another episode of Morgan Freeman's "Through the Worm Hole" (on the Science Channel), I was again fascinated by the notion of time travel. One researcher has discovered that it is possible to send a signal (from one device) to another as the latter picks up the signal slightly before it is actually sent. This was presented as an example of "travel into the past."

However, it occurs to me that from the perspective of the "receiver," it might as well be seen as an example of "travel into the future." Indeed, one experiment in telepathy at a major university asked a human subject to press a lever when a signal was sent—some were very good at this, and some could even anticipate the signal, pressing the lever a split second before the signal was sent. Did these subjects literally travel into the future, sensing the event before it became the "present" in normal space/time?

Now—here is my clincher—if the familiar laws of space/time can be set aside in these various experiments, can they not also offer possible explanations of such things as intuition of coming happenings, premonitions, visions of the "future" in waking or dreaming states?

Unfortunately, the scientists who are working on these issues do not seem to connect their theories with happenings well documented in the storehouse of human experience. There are many such examples, some involving well known historical figures, some involving ordinary people, perhaps those we ourselves know—or even ourselves. How often have you known who is on the phone before you pick it up, or think of someone who then gets in touch shortly thereafter? How often do you dream of something that happens later, including details that were included in the dream (as if time were reversed)? Science seems to disregard all evidence that does not occur in a laboratory under controlled conditions, but we do not live in laboratories, and our lives occur in totally unregulated environments.

And—here is another even more radical theory. One of the scientists on Freeman's program commented that if time travel were possible, we would be inundated with visitors from the future. My question: how do we know that these visitors are not already here, living more or less undetected among us, looking and acting pretty much like the rest of humanity? Indeed, how do you know that we—the ones more open, more seemingly "awake," more "sensitive" in ways unfathomable to the "throng"—are not in fact "visitors from the future," infused with ways of perceiving and knowing beyond the comprehension of the "regular folk" who represent the majority among the masses of humanity?

If we are not in fact "visitors from the future" we are certainly partial representatives of the next stage of human evolution, when expanded consciousness will characterize everyone. If nothing else, we are here to point the way, to enable others as they enter this transformed state.

Certainly, those of us who have undergone the extreme transformation of Kundalini are obliged to help others on this particular path. And I believe that the bliss state that Kundalini can awaken is in fact the state that all will enter as future humans.

I am not insisting that any of these notions is true. But Freeman's program does awaken speculation on some central issues—in particular, how it is that the "two tribes" of humanity are so different from one another in so many ways?

ABOUT INTENTION

There seems to be a great deal of discussion these days about "intention." Apparently, the idea is to set your intention for whatever it is you want and then it will come to you. One man decided he wanted a million dollars, so he pasted a copy of a million dollar bill over his bed so he would see it first thing each morning. He did get his million—in fact, he made many millions through a popular book he wrote, and bought himself a multi-million dollar house and fancy cars.

Now, I have nothing against "asking the universe" for what you need, but I am mystified that so many seem to think the technique is to be used to gain excessive material wealth. Little is said about desiring to be closer to the divine or doing work that is true to one's soul purpose. In fact, it seems that for the most part "god" (the divine, source, reality, ultimate essence, whatever you wish to call it) is simply ignored.

I have indeed asked the universe for things I truly needed in the past. I once got a car this way—not a fancy expensive one, but a "pre-used" model that was quite inexpensive and was perfect for my needs. I also found an ideal apartment when I moved to this new city a year ago— indeed it was the first one I looked at—and I had in fact asked for "outside help" for this.

However, I am not sure we should focus on this technique to the exclusion of other interests and avenues. I feel our best "intention" is to be open to what the universe brings us—whether friends or activities or transcendent meditations or progress on our spiritual path. If we need a new (or any) job, indeed we should ask. If we are hungry, we should ask for food. If we are lonely, we should ask for friends.

But—asking to become a millionaire? Whatever happened to "lay not up treasures on earth"—an admonition once most honored?

My daily prayer is "Give me the strength to do what I am supposed to be doing on this earth and the good sense to know what that is."

I also believe that those of us who have been blessed with Kundalini awakening have already received the greatest possible gift the planet offers, and thus our overall intention should be—surely—to deepen our own spiritual connection and to contribute in whatever way we can to the welfare of the world around us. I see many who do this in various ways—sometimes they drive old cars, wear the same clothes for years, and live in modest houses. Some give through their art or other forms of creativity and service. Some dedicate their own spiritual practices to raising the overall planetary vibration. They are our models and our inspiration.

They bless and are blessed for they understand and practice true dedication.

NICE IS NOT ENOUGH

Last night I went to hear a famous spiritual teacher speak at Grace Cathedral in San Francisco. Grace Cathedral is vast. It holds many hundreds of people and was filled to capacity. I felt honored to be in the company of so many "serious" seekers, persons sufficiently dedicated to the search for spiritual connection that they had come to enjoy this evening of communion together.

The speaker, a major leader in her (Buddhist) tradition, was a very nice person. She spoke calmly and coherently about her topic, which was, essentially, how to avoid feeling aggressive when others confront or insult you. Yet, as her talk unfolded, I began to feel more and more as if I were back in my little Midwestern hometown, hearing a lesson in Sunday school. The emphasis seemed to be on personal psychology. In fact, the presentation was more like a self-help session (how can I deal with my own anger, frustration, lack of self-esteem, resentment, etc.) than an exploration of serious spiritual issues.

The overall effect might be described as "bland." No one could take offense, no one could seriously disagree with the premises. But I kept wondering, whatever happened to the passion of the ancient founders of her lineage? Where was the mystery and intensity of the shamanic tradition from which it derived? Where was the sense of mystical connection as the primary token of authentic spiritual experiences? These comments were recipes for social interaction, not revelations of the divine. Whatever became of ecstasy? Where was transcendence?

Now, instead of bland, what I yearn for is the "passionate intensity" of the awakened mystic. By this, I am not calling for people who become fanatics or zealots, who act out or contrive to insert drama into everyday experience. But I am longing for what the poets, at least, have often sought, a real, deeply felt, totally alive connection with something of great significance beyond the level of the mundane. I am convinced that transcendence is possible, at least in our most splendid moments. Life is not a pleasant game of chess, but a dance full of unexpected turns and movements, all calling us to discover unexplored regions of our own spirit, sometimes involving the extremities of both beatitude and pain.

We face overwhelming problems in our world. We need daring leadership, persons of integrity and fierce vision for whom "nice" is not enough. We need to open ourselves to what T. S. Eliot called, "the awful daring of a moment's surrender." For many of us, Kundalini offers such a moment, such an opportunity of surrender.

THE STAGES OF BELIEF

I am trying to construct a paradigm to help understand the various stages and varieties (or at least some) of religious/spiritual belief. What I have come up with is tentative, at best, and is not intended to be a final classification or description.

1. The beginning stage is that of unquestioning belief. This level embraces various groups, from the naive primitive accepting the worship practices of the tribe, to the true believer in modern society, who accepts the authority of his received tradition, without challenging or confronting its premises. The obedient followers of the "church" (of whatever stripe) as well as the "born agains" of certain traditions fall here. These represent those who long for authority to bequeath them a final truth, a boon that requires no effort of mental scrutiny on their part.

Truth at this stage is very simple. All is divided into black vs. white, good vs. evil, and us vs. them. These often consider themselves the chosen ones, and some in contemporary times insist that the end of the world will soon occur, themselves being the sole remnant to be "saved." Often these folks are very good people individually—they will help you in your need, succor you when you are ill, etc. But their credo brooks no violation of enshrined belief or prescribed code of behavior.

2. There are those who have outgrown or renounced their early heritage, and have found nothing to replace it with. Some rank high on the intellectual scale. Often they become the "scoffers and skeptics," who belittle and deride anyone who takes seriously the spiritual search or the actuality of the divine. They are in fact very hurt by their loss of an earlier idealism, the loss which lurks in their consciousness as a kind of betrayal. They defend themselves by their scorn.

Another category of the "disillusioned idealist" includes many of the great contributors to overall social good. These have lost their early naive faith, and now commit themselves to the betterment of human kind, actually enacting the precepts of most religious systems without embracing the philosophy. They are the "secular humanists," who so disturb the committed believers.

3. Yet another group consists of those who still grieve consciously for the loss of their original faith, now lost forever. They yearn for some sort of renewed commitment, but have found none.

4. And still another segment turns from "religion" in the traditional sense to "spirituality" as framed by many of the New Age adherents. Often these categorically reject all systems which emphasize the negatives—suffering, pain, and the possibility of personal disaster—and insist that reality has no shadow. All is love and light at every moment, and to verify this, just think it so.

5. A final category embraces those who, by some miracle of grace, transcend these earlier mind states and find a basis for belief, though the underlying premise of this conviction may never be spelled out in full. This is the high mystic path, founded on a stable mental foundation, which neither rejects nor insists on its own claims for authenticity, but follows the dictates of the heart. These possess, in Thoreau's words, an "innocence purified by experience." They are neither utterly naive nor totally disillusioned. They are firm in their faith that "something is there," and serve as both observer and recipient of the gifts such awareness brings.

To arrive at this state may take a lifetime of yearning and preparation. No one can bestow it on another. A major life transforming experience may evoke such transfiguration. Yet more and more are reporting such awakenings, which some tie to the ongoing evolution of consciousness.

Is Kundalini the engine of such transfiguration of consciousness? To doubt after extreme transcendent awareness becomes near impossible. Certainly, the Kundalini experience carries one to a new level of perception, of conviction, and of gratitude, all flowing from the experience of unconditional love at the cellular level. But no one can yet fully explain the mechanism or meaning of the Kundalini transformation. This, I think, is the true definition of the mystical experience—it offers proof on the level of the subjective response that which no assault of intellect can diminish or destroy. Blessed are those who reach this state, for they know a reality beyond questioning, for theirs is a "self-validating experience."

THE GIFT OF EL COLLIE

When I experienced awakening in 1981, I knew only one person who had even heard of Kundalini. For the most part, I kept silent about my own experience—it was mysterious, exotic, esoteric in the extreme. A few books were available, but for the most part it was a very solitary journey. Some years later, I asked a friend (who knew about such things as the internet, which was itself still a novelty) to type in the word kundalini to see what came up. I was thrilled when four references appeared. For me, it was as though the most hidden and indeed ultra-secret realms were coming to light. Today, if you type in that word on Google, you will get literally thousands of references—Kundalini awareness seems to have swept across the planet like a great wave of Awakening.

But in the eighties and early 1990s, such awareness was still quite rare. Thus, when I heard that someone in Oakland (California) had started a newsletter dedicated entirely to Kundalini awakening, I was overjoyed. It was called *Shared Transformation* and was written and edited by El Collie, along with her husband Charles Kress. I immediately subscribed and ordered all back issues. Eventually, I submitted some of my own writings, and was delighted that they were accepted for publication. For me, this was a kind of milestone in my journey, finally sharing publicly what had been, until then, almost exclusively a private experience. Later, El Collie even published some of my poems, and again I was deeply grateful.

Though I never met El Collie, I learned quite a bit about her from the newsletter. She was obviously extremely intelligent, a very articulate and knowledgeable writer on this little known topic. She was able to speak authoritatively on all aspects of the Kundalini journey, from its sources in various traditions to modern applications. She warned us against relying on false teachers, and suggested alternatives to sometimes misleading diagnoses by traditional medical practitioners. She was in fact an encyclopedia of pertinent information, and much of what she said had been tested in her own experience.

In addition to offering her personal reflections, she included the voices of many others undergoing spiritual emergence of various kinds. It was reassuring to discover that Kundalini awakening was indeed part of a "shared transformation," and she served as the shaman/wise woman assisting others on this difficult journey.

One of the great disappointments of my life was that I never got to meet her in person. I was shocked to discover that she had left the planet before I met her. Her health had continued to deteriorate through the years, bringing ever-increasing pain into her body. I happened recently on one of the last e-mails I received from her, in which she stated that she had carpal tunnel syndrome not only in her hands but in her feet as well. This development must have been devastating for her, for her writing clearly was her lifeblood, the necessity that gave her life fulfillment and purpose.

Her husband and soul mate, Charles, played a major role in the publication of *Shared Transformation*, from its origins as a print publication to its later reemergence as an Internet site. After El Collie's death, Charles did something impressive as a tribute to El Collie and a gift to her friends and audience. He edited and posted online the book she had been working on for years. From reading this amazing manuscript, I learned even more about the life of this fascinating woman. (She never wanted her book to be published by a conventional publisher. She wanted it to be on the Internet, available free to all readers.)

El Collie had always been a pioneer. Disdaining elitism, she identified with those who struggle to survive in our society. She deliberately chose not to go to college (this despite her obvious innate intelligence). She lived a life of adventure. Her early chapters describe how she and her children lay on the floor of their apartment to avoid the gunfire that erupted in the riots in Detroit during the stormy early days of the civil rights movement. She lived in Haight-Ashbury during its heyday as a counterculture center, and participated in many of the social experiments taking place there at that time. She was a feminist poet early on in the Bay Area, and did many public readings at coffee houses and the like. She firmly believed that poetry was part of the oral tradition, and should be heard rather than read.

Thus it was not surprising that this woman of strong conviction and pure intent should be one of the first to offer support for the awakening

Kundalini community. She did not simply dream about the need for new means of connection, she threw herself into the effort to create something utterly novel, totally unfamiliar. For, though such experiences as near-death and out-of-body states were now fairly familiar, Kundalini was still part of the mysterious unknown, totally out of the mainstream consciousness.

And, as always, she did not seek to make significant financial gain from her endeavors. She charged only a minimum amount for the publication, and received little or nothing for her services.

For me, she was that rarity of rarities, a true human being. She was not afraid to take risk. She threw herself fully into her chosen commitments. She lit a path for the rest of us to follow at a time when such mentors were few and near impossible to locate.

Her photograph (online) reveals a tall, imposing woman, with strength and courage inscribed on her face. She would be an indomitable leader and a daunting opponent for those whose principles were suspect. She was, in fact, a goddess, with all the beauty and majesty that that implies. She was the wise Athena, the woman who gave us an incalculable gift of knowledge and encouragement when we needed it most.

Go to www.elcollie.com to read excerpts from *Branded by the Spirit*, El Collie's remarkable autobiography, as well as her astute discussions of the Kundalini process. This site also includes some back issues of *Shared Transformation*.

Recently, I was at an organizational meeting for a small group of women who were planning to meet informally from time to time to enjoy mutual spiritual support. Some felt we should begin by setting a clear intention and then describing how we would achieve it. Some felt we should define aims and means. Then it was suggested that it might be useful for each of us to start with the phrase, "My intention for this group is. . ." and then to finish with whatever came up. Immediately, the following came into my head:

"My intention is to have no intention. My goal is to have no goal. My aim is to forego all aims. I wish to be a seed dropped from above, taking root where it falls, not certain of its true identity until it blossoms in due season."

Of course, such a philosophy ("the path is the goal") may work better at my stage of life than for a twenty- or thirty-year old just beginning the journey. And perhaps some guidelines or general outlines are needed for a group effort.

But, for me, detailed life plans and extensive lists of intended accomplishments have proved futile, since those events which most shaped my experience have frequently come unexpectedly, without apparent design or forewarning. True, I often found that I had unknowingly prepared for the new revelation or unexpected opportunity, sometimes for years. But there was simply no way I could have imagined the form it would take. It often felt as though a "hidden script" unfolded at the propitious moment, bringing a fortuitous meeting or a chance confluence of circumstances which totally altered the course of my life. Who can predict the moment a stranger may appear who totally changes everything? Who could arrange the precise pattern of events that bring transformation?

AWAKENING OSIRIS

Today, I stood at my bookshelf, opened a volume, and my eye fell on these paragraphs from Awakening Osiris: The Egyptian Book of the Dead, translated by Normandi Ellis. This magnificent book is an eloquent, delightfully poetic work, which I read frequently for the beauty of its language and the deep profundity of its text.

This day I am with you. Stabbed by the light of the great mind I wake. The sun crests the hill and the hawk, according to a higher will, whirls and circumscribes day. I am called from my house. I shuffle sand underfoot, but my heart leaps. I open, am pierced by light. A cry escapes my lips. I know not what I say; it is the language of soul beneath skin, the song of birds in acacia trees.

Beautiful is the golden seed from which the corn arises; beautiful the sun on the hill from which springs god's day. My body nourishes some unfolding time and purpose. I shine bronze as Hathor's mirror. My heart lifts like the sun. Passion and power quiver on the land, casting long shadows...

In some respects, Kundalini is itself an "Awakening of Osiris." Indeed, Osiris may be thought of as "the god within."

Once awakened (brought into consciousness) the heart is indeed "pierced by light" and the world and its elements are kissed into luminous radiance.

KUNDALINI AND THE ARTIST

What is the relationship of Kundalini and creative expression? Some believe that Kundalini is often the hidden source of both inspiration and the vital energy which together enable the artist to transcend familiar human limits in new vision and insight.

When we look at the writers of the present as well as the past century, we see many who reached great heights in their achievements and whose works lit up landscapes which were desolate and void of meaning. Loneliness and despair, isolation and meaninglessness are key themes of the modern era. It is as though their brilliance brought them to the very edge of revelation, but kept them from making the final step into affirmation. I think of these as the finest exemplars of the "old consciousness," a refined awareness that has not undergone the transmutation wrought by the alchemy of Kundalini.

Above all, Kundalini brings us hope. In the moment of awakening, and through the tokens of love which follow, we no longer question but believe. We are renewed in the fires of our own inner transformation, and even if not all our questions are answered nor all our issues resolved, we no longer cling to despair and disbelief as the only acceptable responses to the human condition. We take off our armor of skepticism and exist with expanded vision, renewed certitude and hope.

Jorge Luis Borges (1899–1986) is one of the great master writers of the past century. His work is dazzling in its effect, and impressive as a giant accomplishment. A perpetual seeker, he never finds the "solution" he obsessively desires. His central image is the labyrinth (of mind, of spirit, of time and history) of which he is captive. This, along with a never ending obsession with death and the brevity of human life, are his persistent themes. His vision is vast, but for whatever reason, he never relinquishes his despair.

Indeed, it sometimes seems as though despair were a prerequisite for any artist working today, apparently as an expression of the lostness and dislocation felt by many in the world today. Sometimes the works seem to lack any coherent meaning, and come across as "mental doodling" or pointless scribbles.

Kundalini reveals that joy is available, even amidst the surrounding chaos. It offers a sense of meaning and connection, for transcendence does not depend on the vagaries of the outer world.

A CROSS-CULTURAL ENCOUNTER

I was there to have my income tax return filled out. She was the accountant assigned to my file. She was a motherly looking woman in her late forties or early fifties. She was rather short and plump, had a slightly dark complexion, and abundant jet black hair that hung down around her shoulders. I studied her face with interest, and noted the gold bangles on her wrist. She spoke English with ease, but she had an unmistakable accent that at first I could not place.

Then it came to me. She was not Hispanic, as I had first assumed—she was Indian (from India) and in fact carried a profile similar to those often depicted in early Indian art.

So I asked her what her nationality was, and she answered that she was in fact from Bangalore, one of the technological centers of this rapidly developing country. She had been fascinated by numbers since she was quite young, and had majored in accounting, ultimately taking a master's degree in an American university. She was here because her husband, also Indian, had been transferred to this pleasant mountain town, which also was a high tech center in its own right.

As we talked, and as she continued with my tax preparation, I thought how ironic it was that she, who came from the land of the ancient rishis and yogic saints, the repository of almost magical ancient lore and practices, now epitomized the new age, where the young were now trained early in the intricacies of the "new mysticism," high tech with its own hierarchy of priests and gurus, its skilled practitioners and its no-nonsense views which had no room for the ancient gods and their myths and rites. And I suspected that, for her, the old divinities and their ceremonies and legends, the sounds of the sacred language of Sanskrit spoken or chanted, the subtle movements of hand or body to raise and circulate the inner energies—these were now dead forms, long since emptied of meaning or usefulness, relics of an obsolete era.

And here I sat opposite her, I as one who had never even traveled to that wondrous far off land, but who had again and again felt the power of

Shiva and his feminine form as Shakti, who knew through intuition and seeming remembrance, how to evoke the ancient forms, who had felt the wonder of the energy known as Kundalini in her own body many times over.

It seemed the supreme irony, as if ancient and contemporary were changing places, and the world of the old had been replaced by the face of the new, and vice versa.

When I left, I thanked her, and mentioned that I had a niece who lived in Dallas, where she had lived before coming here. She smiled and answered politely, "Everyone has relatives who live in Dallas."

JAN FRAZIER: *WHEN FEAR FALLS AWAY*

I have been reading an engrossing book called When Fear Falls Away, by Jan Frazier. Jan experienced a sudden "awakening" in 2003, when her fear, her dread, her anxiety simply vanished, as if she had molted or shed a skin she no longer needed. Again and again, she wept tears of joy, sometimes mingling the wetness flowing from her eyes with the rain itself, as if the two were together the evidence of the ceaseless flow of the waters of creation.

She does not (at least in the portion I have read thus far) mention Kundalini but rather speaks of joy, happiness, delight in all that surrounds her. What brought about this sudden reversal in her life? She explains that for the first time she asked for help from "somewhere," not knowing who or what it was she was "praying" to. At that very moment, she felt a kind of "dancing" around her head, as if someone were whirling around her in circles, clapping hands, laughing.

This was, in Katherine Anne Porter's words, the "moment that changes everything."

Fortunately, Jan was a teacher of creative writing, and thus was able to shape her experience into a beautifully written work of art. Her imagery is striking, and adds a special richness to her telling, the way hidden treasures (currents, nuts) yield delight to a fruit cake that is otherwise rather plain.

One of the most striking features (for me) is her descriptions of her personal experiences that in fact are reflections of universal aspects of the journey. And I recognized in her account many similarities to my own transformation, expressions of the same dilemmas and delights, sometimes as virtually identical responses.

Jan, as a writer and teacher of writing, is determined to describe her experience fully and accurately, yet—and this is the great irony—what is happening to her—this intense inner experience of joy and freedom from fear—is by its own nature indescribable. How can you delineate those inner currents, those wondrous waves of feeling that have taken over your psyche and now sweep you along in a tumultuous rapture? By definition, these subjective states are ineffable. As well try to catch the wind in a butterfly net or look for god in a petri dish as capture these indefinable states in words.

She also enters what mystics call the experience of Oneness, the realization that all of our perceptions, based as they are on the separation of one thing from another, one creature or item from all the rest, are false, for we are all—every person and sentient being and even the non-aware components of our world—part of a wholeness, a single unity. She uses the term "sponginess" to describe the porous and permeable quality of reality.

Jan includes as well an eloquent description of a glorious sexual experience with her husband. Often, when spirit awakens, flesh is filled with great joy that then expresses itself as sex on a new level, reaching what many would call ultimate Tantric experience. It often feels as if the gods and goddesses have come to earth and imbued oneself and the partner with divine attributes. Jan does not speak in such terms, but rather writes with grace and wonder of the event itself as transcendence beyond past pleasures.

And then there is the happiness, the constant euphoria, of her new found state. She not only is relieved of her past anxieties and fear, but realizes that she has found the strength and stability to face any challenge that may arise in her life. She is, in fact, now a new being, for she has literally been "reborn."

So far I have read only the first section of the book, but I am delighted to discover so many parallels with my own and others' experience as we move ahead on our personal journeys of transformation. Though universal in its overall scope, each voyage is at the same time new, each telling fresh, for each is a unique encounter with the mystery that takes us back to source.

(Out my window, I see that the March snow has stopped, at least for now. The temperature is 37 degrees, so it should melt in a day or two. It is still a "winter wonderland" outside. I am warm and cozy in my apartment looking out on the beauty without, as if someone had dropped a lovely white silk shawl over the trees and landscape.)

CAN A COMPUTER CHANGE YOUR LIFE?

Can a new computer change your life? My answer is yes. I am totally immersed in learning to use this new device, and am in fact rather dazzled by all it can do. For me it is a great boon to be able to enlarge the type (on most documents), to move easily up and down the page, and so forth. The computer also offers voice over (haven't tried it yet), a web cam (haven't tried this either), an incredible speaker system, and so forth. Now I realize that I was trying to drive a model T when everyone else was driving a Ferrari.

And, as I mulled over this (for me) dramatic transition, I realize that I have witnessed many such changes in technology in my life. I learned to type on an old-fashioned Underwood typewriter, then came the electric typewriter, then IBM Selectric (with its magical correction key, which meant we no longer had to use carbon paper and white out for our student papers, nor for our own articles and dissertations), then the early computers (the early Macs were small white boxes with tiny screens), and so forth.

I am always slow to catch on to the new technology, and typically learn about things long after everyone else has gone far ahead. But I do love this new machine.

I have always been a "word person" so this new addition to my life is very meaningful. In particular the new screens and the capacity to reverse the colors from black text on white background to the opposite of white text on black background make for much less eyestrain. For this reason alone I recommend this model for anyone with special vision problems. For the first time in many years, I am not going to bed with eyestrain.

And, I might also add that I have also seen many changes in public awareness of Kundalini over the years. In 1981, the year of my awakening, I knew no one who had even heard of Kundalini. Now it has in effect become a buzz word, and more and more people are—it seems—having their own awakening experiences. Kundalini sites are numerous on the Internet and a great store of information is readily available. Kundalini, has indeed come "out of the closet" and now is an exoteric rather than an esoteric topic for many.

Have you ever entered a bookstore and felt a sudden wave of joy flash through your body? It is as if the books actually emanated a special vibration that your inner detector could receive even before you absorbed the contents.

In earlier times, books were considered sacred, for they carried the power of the gods passed down to humanity. The Shaiva Sutras, for example, connect us to ancient wisdom coming down from supernal forces, for parts of this book are thought to be the product of divine inspiration. In the Christian world, monks labored for years to provide through their illuminated manuscripts an appropriate home for the sacred texts of the Bible. Probably these early volumes carried discernible vibrations of their makers as well as their contents. Long before printing, books were carefully inscribed on papyrus or vellum or other materials to preserve such knowledge received from above.

And—strangely enough—even the books of today, including the paperbacks, if they are on sacred topics, radiate a special energy, which we may sense if we attend closely.

This morning, I felt no special energies moving as I started my practice, and decided that I would simply go through my chi gong exercises as a form of stretching and exercise. But at some point, I was moved to walk over to my bookcase and stand before a shelf of Kundalini texts. And at that point, I felt what Vyaas Houston calls a "brightening" of various chakras, almost as if the books were speaking to me, saying, "Yes, we hold sacred knowledge and this wisdom spreads outward in energetic waves to those who approach with a right attitude."

At that point, one book suddenly stood out. It was entitled Mudras, an area I have not given much attention to recently. I opened it and formed one of the simplest of all mudras, thumb against first two fingers, and as I did so I felt the energies move in subtle delight.

Always, there is new experience, a different mode to explore. The Kundalini trail is never dull.

THE FULL MOON AND INNER ENERGIES

Have you noticed anything different in your life and in your field during the full moon? I have. For some reason, the inner energies, which have sometimes remained almost dormant for many weeks, can be aroused again. Then once more I am in that place where every movement of hand or arm awakens into light. Each breath is a blessing—of love energy, always almost too much to bear.

What I describe happens almost exclusively (for me) during my morning "practice." (This consists at this time of bowing before Buddha—as a thangka—then slow movement, with a bit of *chi gong* included, sometimes to music, sometimes in silence.) What I want is to FEEL the inner connection, the link to the divine, to reaffirm that I and it are one, for I exist only as a part of It. Words and thoughts all drop away at this time. I do not wish to "control" my mind, but to follow it, to allow it to lead me into ever higher expressions of divine unity.

This is my way of helping to raise the vibrations of the planet itself—I think many of us are participating in this process. We know who we are, and we are certain that this "assignment" is why we are here.

And we are immensely grateful to be included in this process.

P. S. The music for what is often my morning dance can be found at www.nandhi.com, as The Dance of the Siddhas (Turiya Nada) included in "The Cave of the Siddhars." The text on this site is also fascinating (to me, anyway).

KUNDALINI AND CREATIVITY

Like many creative geniuses, Beethoven (1770–1827) seemed possessed by a brain that was "on fire." His level of functioning in terms of his productivity was so far beyond the "normal" that to the ordinary person he might seem "crazed" or suffering from some rare form of madness. Certainly he was obsessed, and this was part of the price he had to pay for his massive gift. And "the boy" he mentioned was his nephew, possibly the only love object in Beethoven's life until even he too rejected his eccentric uncle and left the composer to cope alone with his growing deafness and isolation.

Likewise such geniuses as Mozart, Bach, and Picasso as well Jung and Einstein, Shakespeare, and Dante appeared to possess a creative energy so intense that it in effort "forced" them to produce masterworks of art or science well beyond the capacity of the "ordinary human."

Often these creators work feverishly on their projects, sometimes forgoing sleep or adequate sustenance to complete their works. They possess and are possessed by energies that appear to fuel and direct their efforts.

Is such fervent outpouring the result of sublimated Kundalini? Many think so, and indeed there is reason to suspect a connection between Kundalini and creativity.

RECONCILING THE OPPOSITES

In order to complete initiation, we must discover a way—or become possessed by a way—to reconcile the opposites. Yet, all around us, on personal and transpersonal levels, in private and cosmic realms, the evidence piles up that the split between the disparates continues to widen, moving toward a seemingly irreconcilable rift.

Consider, for example, Bliss and the Shadow. I myself have known a good deal of bliss in my life. In meditation, in movement, in group energy experiences—in yoga, in breathing, in holding —often a rapture flows. I am "ravished by the god," I enter a realm of such deep sensuous delight in which I forget that I am a mere mortal, subject to the contingencies of the everyday. I become nothing but bliss awareness. I am ananda, ananda is my self and substance.

But then I awaken. I come back to "reality" and find myself, once again, in the "real world" (then California), at the center of ever recurring catastrophe. Here the ground roars and opens beneath your very feet; giant sheets of fire incinerate not just houses but people, neighborhoods, entire communities. Cars pile up in massive collisions on fog darkened freeways, floods threaten cities in the south.

And all around us is evidence of such individual suffering as we had not dreamt of. Mothers with children in arms beg in the street, human wrecks huddle on sidewalks, old women wrap themselves in blankets against the cold as they curl up in doorways.

The transgressions of government and various national and international institutions are too familiar to catalogue. Powerful commercial interests poison air, water, or soil, as common citizens wonder what to do; these same interests loot the national treasury through various schemes, all serving the interests of the very, very rich. Great profits are reaped by the munitions manufacturers, the pharmaceutical industries, the banking sectors. We are fed obvious untruths and propaganda in the service of special interests. When the press tries to expose the truth, they are accused of printing "fake news."

The airways are filled with indecencies unimaginable in a previous age. Our language is polluted with what used to be thought of as obscenities. Our children absorb and reflect the false values inculcated by the TV screen and the movie theaters. Our leaders display such vulgarity and power lust, such disdain for fact and truth that democracy itself is threatened. Unimaginable terror groups commit atrocities against innocent citizens.

And so it goes. Evidence of the Shadow—of universal disintegration of values and behavior, of recurrent disaster—is massive on all levels, personal, public, and cosmic. Each day reveals its new scenario of grief, of suffering, of massive corruption and decay. And yet—each time we return to that deep center, each instant we make contact with that something which convinces that we have not yet discovered who we truly are—we are filled again with a bliss which whispers of that which exists beyond suffering. We know that we are linked to an inscrutable power which pervades our consciousness and carries our body to near insupportable levels of rapture. We feel that here, in this way, abiding in this reality, we once again verify the ever present bond between human and divine, phenomenal world and source, striving and being.

But this—the Transcendent Moment and the Contingent Universe, Universal Love and Private Suffering—is but the first of many oppositions. Consider, also, Ecstasy (the bliss of total union with the invisible) and Normal Awareness (the familiar consciousness that governs and orders our lives in all our "mundane" states of being). We live, alternately, in two worlds—the world of being and the world of knowing, the absolute realm of conceptless awareness and the idea-ridden universe of daily life. In the former, we suspend not only awareness but judgment and critical faculty. In the latter, we explore the ideational realm, we contemplate, weigh, measure, and judge. We challenge and correct.

The exercise of the rational faculty is essential to our well being. It saves us from charlatans and protects us from the false gods, whether secular or sacred. But—how much easier was the task of the saints in their cells, the hermits in their mountain caves—how much simpler to embrace a single, coherent vision of truth, to remain fixed in perpetual bliss, rather than being pressed to travel constantly between the two realms, now flooded with bliss of union, now challenging the very evidence of one's own experience. We are neither saints nor skeptics, neither committed sectarians nor scornful disbelievers. We are explorers, vacillating constantly between the two domains (one holy, one profane), as if our brains were a condo leased to separate tenants on a "time share" basis. When one is in residence, the other must be absent. They know of each other's presence only by notes left on the refrigerator or taped to the telephone.

And we could continue our list of antinomies: Universal Love and Private Grief; Evolution of Consciousness vs. evidence of a Disintegrating Society. We could consider the oppositions inherent in the many potential approaches to and interpretations of "reality"—as obtained through the perspectives of body wisdom, mind sense, societal issues, depth psychology, art, music, poetry, movement, etc. Each conveys a conviction of truth in the paradigm it embodies, but none offers a totally comprehensive or totally convincing vision. (The bodyworker, for example, discovers a "storehouse of the past" carried in the body's own tissues and cells, and effects a seeming cure; the astronomer constructs a cosmic record from far more abstract evidence. Each embraces an aspect of truth, but none offers a complete perspective.)

Again, there are the many layers and levels of consciousness that have unfolded in history, with its many competing world views and modes of perception. We cannot reenter the ancient shaman's world, even as it beckons. For all we know, it—or another equally "primitive" mode— may have been the true entryway, a window opening onto reality itself, a vision now lost to us forever.

And there is the dichotomy of the immutable other (god? emanation? higher self? the transcendent?) and the shape changer within. For we, in our most private and essential nature, are never at rest—we are moody, distraught, joyous, and calm, all within a single day—or hour. We ourselves perpetually shift, now exultant, now sad, now caught in reflection, now swept by passionate feeling. The divine melody may be fixed in eternity, but we, the instruments, are called to play many variations on the score.

Yet each time we return to that deep center, each instant we make contact with that awareness that convinces us that there is ever more to discover about our source and who we truly are—we are filled again with a bliss that whispers of that which lies beyond the state of suffering and grief. We know we are linked to an inscrutable power that infuses and animates our own selves and often carries us to near unsupportable levels of rapture.

We realize that here, in this way, abiding in this reality, we once more verify the immutable bond between human and divine, world and source. (from *Unmasking the Rose: A Record of a Kundalini Initiation*)

ABOUT ARTIFICIAL INTELLIGENCE
AND ULTIMATE TRUTH (SATCITANANDA)

I wrote the following last night after reading an article by a respected pioneer researcher and inventor in the field of consciousness, matter, and energy.

I am neither a mathematician nor a scientist. But for many years I have been intrigued by the ideas emerging from the ongoing discoveries of the new physics, including the recent theories pertaining to AI. Although I have not read these reports with any degree of sophistication, I have perused them with interest and attention and indeed these novel concepts have provoked in me certain responses, which I summarize below.

My main concern (to go the heart of the matter) is that AI, no matter how it is presented, does not include feeling. Concepts do not include feeling. Notions do not have feeling. Ideas themselves do not have feelings. Devices that replicate rational human thought processes do not have feelings.

Thus, when we posit "consciousness" as a basic aspect of reality, we omit an essential component—indeed the essence–of that awareness that reveals "who we really are."

Satcitananda:

Satcitananda (an ancient Indian term) represents "existence, consciousness, and bliss" or "truth, consciousness, bliss." It is an epithet and description for the subjective experience of the ultimate, unchanging reality in Hinduism called Brahman. (from Wikipedia).

Sat is existence and of course we exist. *Cit* is consciousness and of course we are conscious (in the usual sense of this word). But what is bliss? Is it merely the joy that we know when we think about the world about us and contemplate its nature? I think it is far more. I believe that this bliss is the core of "great consciousness"—awareness of both the cosmic field of knowingness and human perception of that which informs and sustains the universe.

This is a big claim. But my own experience verifies that when we enter a state in which we experience total, overwhelming, boundless love (as felt in our own blood and veins and cells), then we are in alignment with the universal swirling dynamic and undefinable impulse that powers the universe and all that is in it. This connection can be known only when it is realized internally and individually. It can come about through Kundalini awakening. This realization is known as Awakening or Moksha or Enlightenment in different traditions. We will never think our way to such realizations. God (the ultimate reality, essential source) is not a concept nor a notion nor a thought nor an idea. It is not captured through theories or diagrams or formulations. It is the territory, not the map, the lost treasure unearthed and brought home. It is a felt reality and we can only know it through the coursing of infinite love through our bodies, not as sexual flow but rather as sublimated energy, the source itself transformed and embodied in our own fleshly forms and felt as rapture.

It is like any form of love. It cannot be seen or measured or weighed, yet it is undeniably present, and is validated through the experience itself.

This is why ultimately AI has no final relevance or significance, though it offers interesting material for speculation. It misses the core element, the awareness that is union with divine reality. This state opens us to Oneness and our realization of who we really are—infinitely small vibrating nodes within the body of the vast indefinable, ineffable Source.

WHY AFFIRMATIONS MATTER

I must confess. For years I have been skeptical of the power of affirmations to produce the results attributed to them by many. I simply did not see how saying a few words could create welcome changes merely by repeating them.

Recently I have come to see the role of affirmations very differently. Here is why:

I attended a recent presentation by a well-known energy healer and she gave us an exercise that convinced me I was wrong. Here is the exercise. It is very simple and only takes a few minutes.

First, you hold your hands in front of you. Then you place your palms together, noticing the creases at the base of your palm. You take notice that your hands match in size. Then you select one or the other hand to focus on. You concentrate for a few minutes on making that hand bigger. You envision it growing larger and larger, until it fills the room and then space itself. When you feel you have "made it grow" for enough time, you bring your two palms together again and see if they are still a match.

When I did this, I saw that the fingers on one hand were significantly longer than those of the other. I was amazed.

How did this happen? Clearly there is a very close connection between mind and body. We of course know this already, but for me this was convincing proof.

Now, what about affirmations? Here is some evidence that is also very compelling.

Bruce Lipton has studied the effect of the surrounding environment on blood cells in the laboratory. He finds that when the cells are in a welcoming atmosphere, they literally open up to receive more blood. When the atmosphere is charged with negativity, they close down and no longer receive the same infusion. Thus joy brings better health and depression creates the likelihood of illness.

The work of Emoto on water has broken new ground. He found that when the water crystals were bombarded with negative thoughts, they became distorted and misshapen. When they were given messages of love, they went into symmetrical form, reflecting the consciousness of the observer. Sometimes Emoto just pasted written messages in front of the crystals and the effect was the same.

Peter Tompkins and Christopher Bird did impressive studies of the interactions of human thought and plant reaction in the 70s (*The Secret Life of Plants*). Their work provided clear indications that plants reacted strongly to the consciousness of the human with which they were associated. Thus, when the observer thought of harming or killing the plant, the polygraph reacted strongly. The plant also reacted in a positive way when the experimenter was making love many miles away. Studies also have shown that plants grow more successfully when they are treated with love as well as when music is played for them.

All of these studies together present a convincing picture that thought and frequencies definitely affect "matter," whether the matter is exposed to a human participant or to a nonhuman source.

My conclusion: yes, our affirmations can and do affect us, in ways that are just now beginning to be understood. Thought does create reality and intention does influence results.

(My only caveat here is that there seem to be limits to what our own personal thoughts can achieve, particularly when we move to a more universal and global level. But who knows what we might achieve if we band together to produce planet wide peace and love.)

ANCIENT WISDOM AND MODERN SCIENCE

For some time I have watched with interest as the New Physics circles around and now back to the beginning point, where ancient wisdom resides. Consider, for example, the view of the nature of matter held by contemporary science and the ancient teachers of India known as rishis.

For centuries, science held that matter was indeed "hard stuff," difficult to penetrate, palpable and real. Then, as time passed, science discovered that matter was made of atoms, which were held to be indestructible bits of a universal substance, the foundation materials of the material universe. Then—voila!—science learned that atoms were "cuttable" after all. (The word "atom" is derived from the Greek "a" (not) plus the verb for "cut.") Indeed, it was proclaimed that atoms were mostly empty space, like an orange in a football field.

Most recently, physicists have put forward the notion of "String Theory," which is very hard to understand. But string theory does not refer to long strings of whatever, as we might suppose. It posits that atoms themselves, those infinitesimal bits which compose everything we label "matter," are composed of tiny "strings" which vibrate like the strings of a violin. The infinite atoms of the universe all vibrate at various ratios, creating the symphony of the universe.

What we think of as the "real world" is thus an illusion, something our brains create given the stimuli which impinge on our senses. It is, in fact, a field of dancing electric charges which lack mass or material substance.

In ancient yogic and Buddhist lore, we learn that the world is not as it seems, that it is in fact an illusion which we mistake for the reality. This illusion is called "Maya," the veil which covers all of creation, so that we do not perceive the reality resting behind. The "illusion" includes not only things but the processes of the social world. Our grasping for wealth, material success, social position, fame and such—all are produced from "maya," the mistaken notions which delude our spirits. Truth is not to be found in externals (samsara), but in the interior world where our souls can link with the higher reality (nirvana).

Furthermore, certain ancient schools posited vibration itself as the basis of the universe. Here is an excerpt from an article on Wikipedia on Kashmiri Shaivism:

SPANDA

"The Spanda system, introduced by Vasugupta (c. 800 AD), is usually described as 'vibration/movement of consciousness'. Abhinavagupta uses the expression 'some sort of movement' to imply the distinction from physical movement; it is rather a vibration or sound inside the Divine, a throb. The essence of this vibration is the ecstatic self-recurrent consciousness.

The central tenet of this system is 'everything is Spanda', both the objective exterior reality and the subjective world. Nothing exists without movement, yet the ultimate movement takes place not in space or time, but inside the Supreme Consciousness. So, it is a cycle of internalization and externalization of consciousness itself, relating to the most elevated plane in creation (Śiva-Śakti Tattva).

The most important texts of the system are the *Śiva Sutras, Spanda Karikas* and *Vijñāna Bhairava Tantra*."

A similar notion is found in Plato's myth of the cave, where people sit and stare at shadows on the wall, not realizing that the source of the shadows lies outside and they are confusing the appearance for reality.

Another example is the thought from Christian Science, which proclaims: "There is no life, truth, intelligence or substance in matter, for all is Infinite Mind and its Infinite Manifestation, for god is all in all."

More and more, contemporary thinkers in science are considering mind itself as the Source, for other theories are simply falling apart. Once Divine Consciousness is accepted as the essential premise, all else comes into place.

My favorite reading in this area (of ancient wisdom) comes from the writings of Jai Deva Singh (translator and commentator) and one of my favorite books is *The Yoga of Delight, Wonder, and Astonishment: A Translation of the Vijnana-Bhairava* (Suny Series in Tantric Studies) with an introduction by Paul Muller-Ortega. Another is the *Spanda Karikas*, again from the Suny Series and with an introduction by Paul Muller-Ortega. ("Karikas" means commentaries on and "Spanda" is throb or pulsation.) And I realize that much of my grasp (however limited) of these works is based on his (to me) most striking introductory comments. There are other editions of this text, but they derive from various earlier translations, and read like totally different works.)

This edition of the Spanda Karikas is now available on Amazon for a reasonable price. You can also find copies of "The Shiva Sutras" in second hand stores. These are not easy reading, but they contain amazing information, all received by the ancient rishis from other worldly sources (I accept this interpretation, because no other makes sense.)

Here are some comments by Muller-Ortega that stand out, and in fact seem to me to be associated with several of the concepts presented in the more recent work "The Field" by Lynne McTaggart (which, along with other books written for the lay audience, I must rely on for my scattered knowledge of what may be coming up in current concepts of field theory, including the rejection of the big bang theory for a more comprehensive vision of a vast plasma field connecting everything in the cosmos).

"Long before the discoveries of modern physics, the Shaivite concept of spanda intimates a view of reality as composed of a vibratory web of infinite complexity."

(Muller-Ortega continues going into the metaphysical implications.... most physics hasn't reached this point yet):

"Moreover, the Shaivite tradition suggests to us a unifying continuity between our physical reality, the activities of sense perception, and all forms of interior awareness. All of these are seen as phenomenal manifestations of the ultimate consciousness, enmeshed in a complex vibratory matrix."

Muller once more summarizes the text:

"Employing a variety of metaphors, the tradition often glosses the spanda by the term *sphurra*, the scintillating pulse of the supreme light which continuously trembles with its own incandescence. In sonic terms, the spanda is glossed as the nada, the subtle but powerful resonance that echoes through the supreme silence...."

(Now, more extension into metaphysics): "The supreme spanda releases a vibrating spectrum of energies that originate within the supreme (anuttara). As the infinitely fast vibration of the supreme systematically coalesces and condenses into progressively slower and thicker vibrations, tangible perceptible forms emerge from the void and formlessness of the ultimate consciousness. These apparently solid appearances are called 'cognitions' (*puramasa*) and they are complex and sustained interference patterns which arise in the inter-merging cross-swirl of energies created by the interaction of the vibratory consciousness with itself." (Is this the Buddhist "emptiness is form, form is emptiness"?)

Admittedly, these are difficult concepts to grasp. But we can glean what is more or less the gist of such profound and even abstruse comments:

1. What some call god is here called "the supreme."

2. The supreme vibrates first in an "infinitely fast vibration" in a setting void of forms.

3. Gradually it slows and as it does so forms begin to emerge.

4. These become "apparently" solid entities. These arise from "interference patterns" created by the interaction of vibratory consciousness with itself.

Some of these insights have come down to us through various channels and perhaps are not that strange to us. Thus, it is often posited that matter is frozen energy. That is to say, matter vibrates at a much slower rate than other "energies" such as subatomic particles, which are so fast in their vibratory action that we can barely detect them (if at all).

All of this seems to me to have a bearing on Kundalini, unlikely as that may seem. I believe that when we go into altered states such that we can experience inner bliss, we are (literally) vibrating at a higher rate than our "norm." When we return to familiar consciousness, we are moving back into our regular, lower rate of vibration.

The majority of people continue to vibrate at the slower level, and are not aware of the possibilities of "higher vibration consciousness." Kundalini (and perhaps other varieties of altered consciousness) takes us into a higher vibrational state—and this state of enhanced vibration is what the next stage of human evolution is all about.

Another parallel between ancient and modern perspectives has to do with theories of the nature of space. Today, we are told that space is formed by a slight bend in the overall fabric of the universe. Likewise, in the ancient theory of spanda (vibration) we learn that in the beginnings, there was a slight modification of the pulsation which in turn was the origin of our vibrating universe.

Today, I happened to catch a bit of a TV science program that suggested yet another possible parallel. Two scientists (whose names I did not catch) developed a very complex mathematical formula that would explain the big bang. They posited the notion that two (or possibly three) "branes" (short for "membranes" that represent separate universes) collided, and our universe was the consequence of this cosmic cataclysm (the "big bang") which released huge amounts of energy. However, there was a hitch. According to the implications of the big bang theory, dark energy (still not fully understood) occupies a great deal of the cosmos. The universe expands constantly, and dark energy causes this process to accelerate even faster. At some point, it expands to the point that nothing exists but the void which swallows all matter.

However, this theory leads to the conclusion that our universe is a unique creation, which will in time disappear.

The scientists then developed a further notion—that the universe does not appear and disappear in a single, unique process, but that the cycle of creation and destruction is repeated often, each half of the dyad occupying a vast expanse of time. Other "branes" collide and beget other universes in an infinite process.

Now, again if we turn to ancient Hindu philosophy we find the notion that Brahma (or Brahmas) constantly make and unmake the universe, in infinite cycles of creation and dissolution. Sometimes this process is expressed as Brahma's breath—each out breath brings into being a new universe (lasting for an unimaginably long period of time) and each in breath dissolves that particular creation. The time in which the created universe exists is known as "Brahma's day" and the time of eclipse is known as "Brahma's night." They are of equal duration.

This phenomenon of cyclic creation and destruction events is also explained by Krishna in the *Bhagavad Gita*, here explained by Bibhu Dev Misra:

"Those who understand the cosmic laws know that the Day of Brahma ends after a thousand yugas and the Night of Brahma ends after a thousand yugas. When the day of Brahma dawns, forms are brought forth from the Unmanifest; when the night of Brahma comes, these forms merge in the Formless again. This multitude of beings is created and destroyed again and again in the succeeding days and nights of Brahma."

"Imperishable and Eternal Brahma": from *Day and Night of Brahma: The Evidence from Fossil Records*, by Bibhu Dev Misra

In addition to the ancient Hindus, there are many other early cultures that posit a similar cyclic nature of time. I am neither a cosmological physicist nor a deep scholar of early Hindu thought, so it is possible my notions are full of flaws of various kinds. So please do not assume they are without error. But it does seem that modern science aligns itself more and more with ancient revealed truth. Such speculation is fascinating, and I would love to see more research into the field of "New Physics and Ancient Wisdom."

If we are honest with ourselves, we must conclude that we in fact know very little about the universe and how it works nor of our place and purpose in it. For the most part, we must stumble ahead, grasping a bit of knowledge here, a glimpse of some possible truth there. Science keeps on changing its views and theories. But Kundalini remains the same, always there though manifesting in untold different ways. When we are in Kundalini bliss, we no longer wonder about explanations and notions, but simply allow it to move through our bodies in a yet unexplained way. We must live always in the mystery, knowing that we are indeed connecting to something greater than ourselves, a reality of Love that binds the world together. We will never be able to think our way to god, but we can participate in nature through the ecstatic energies that derive from Source. Descartes famously said, "I think, therefore I am." Eve

Ensler said instead "I feel, therefore I am."

THE ORIGIN, THE MIDDLE, THE END

"I am the object of all knowledge,
father of the world, its mother,
source of all things, impure and
pure, of holiness and horror.

I am the goal, the root, the witness,
home and refuge, dearest friend,
creation and annihilation,
everlasting seed and treasure.

I am the radiance of the sun, I
open or withhold the rain clouds,
I am immortality and
death, am being and non-being.

I am the Self, Arjuna, seated
in the heart of every creature.
I am the origin, the middle,
and the end that all must come to."

(Krishna, speaking to Arjuna, in
The *Bhagavad Gita*,
tr. Stephen Mitchell

SOLAR FLARES AND HUMAN DESTINY

Recently I have become fascinated with the phenomenon of solar flares (massive emissions of energies) and their possible impact on human experience and the overall process of human evolution. I became interested in this topic because I realized that some of my own somatic experiences (such as wooziness, lack of focus, exhaustion, overall pain and discomfort) actually coincided with scientific reports of major solar events occurring in the same time frame. I also found that certain others (persons with high sensitivities) were having similar responses, again at the same time as my own.

For me, these uncomfortable episodes are followed by ecstatic experiences on the next or the following days.

Some mystical writers have suggested that these infusions of solar energies result in raising our own customary frequencies to a higher level, all as part of the process of human evolution.

I have long believed that there could be a "wild card" in the overall process of human transfiguration. I have no proof, but I do believe such is possible and my hunch is that this natural phenomenon could play a significant role.

Check your energies and see if they follow the trajectory of intense solar activity. Ultimately we are all part of this fascinating process, whatever is causing it and wherever it may lead us.

Anything is possible for anyone any time anywhere. When my spontaneous Kundalini awakening occurred in Kansas when it did as it did, it made a believer out of me. A friend of the time suggested that this must have been a "cosmic joke" to occur then under such circumstances. Such awakenings are no longer a joke, but happenings occurring more and more across the globe, often to unsuspecting subjects.

No one knows precisely what all this means or what its ultimate aim is. We must live always in the mystery, and the name of that mystery is Love.

Open to love and let it carry you to our next destination.

ANOTHER WALK IN THE PARK

I am interested in states of consciousness. There is, of course, mystical consciousness (at one with all), and bliss consciousness, and ecstasy and rapture and transcendent consciousness. (And the list continues to include many, many others, including stages of grief, psychic awareness, trance states—who knows how many there are?)

But there is another which is also one of my favorites which I call simply "Nice Day" consciousness. This is the experience which lacks the intensity of the dramatic Kundalini embrace or the joy of romantic love or the pain of personal crisis. It is like the bread that sustains us between desserts, the pleasant encounter with a neighbor or friend which we depend on to give shape and continuity to our daily lives. It is ordinary experience at its most familiar and best expression.

It leads us into a kind of "I'm OK, you're OK" state (once a popular notion). It tells us life is good, even when simple calmness abides. It assures us we don't have to keep on suffering or worrying about whatever it was that has been bothering us, that it is all right to let go and know that things will, in fact, work out—both for us and the world.

Here is such an experience from yesterday morning:

In the Park (San Francisco)

As soon as I stepped outside, I knew that something was different. Instead of the frequent fog and mist of the Sunset District in San Francisco, there was bright blue sky, well defined fleece-like clouds, warm sun. A rare day, I thought, not to be wasted.

Nora and I arrived at the lake about eleven. Some say Nora is four, others think she is two. Nora is black and white, a purebred border collie (well, perhaps with just a tad of husky). She attracts lots of notice wherever she goes, partly from her glistening coat, partly because her eyes don't match (one is blue, one dark.) She, of course, immediately begins to tug on her leash, excited by the smells and sights around her.

The first thing I notice as we step up the small incline to the sidewalk that circles the lake is the grass. It has rained slightly last night, and the grass has a special glow. Its green is fresh, like spring, though it is now October. "Ah," I think, "something like what Walt Whitman must have had in mind when he wrote his famous poem." ("Leaves of Grass")

We start our obligatory circumambulation around the water. The air smells like eucalyptus, strong enough that even I can notice it. It is reassuring, like the scent of a healing herb in an acupuncturist's office.

I like coming here. First of all, you are never unaccompanied for you are always in clear sight of someone or other. There are no dangerous bushes or shrubs to conceal hidden assailants. I have learned that in the city, you must always be vigilant, aware of your surroundings and the people nearby. I have also learned it is extremely dangerous to "space out" when you are walking the city streets. Your purse could be quickly snatched, or a car whizzing around a corner could harm or annihilate you. In others words, mystical consciousness is dangerous.

This is Stow Lake in Golden Gate Park. The light and the crisp fall air remind me somehow of my visit to Walden Pond, which I finally got to see just one year ago. Walden is a little bigger. I was there in autumn, and indeed the gods had scattered their golden coins along the paths to Thoreau's little abode. The place where Thoreau had built his cabin was clearly marked. Indeed, it was tiny—no wonder he had no room for visitors.

Stow Lake is not in the wilderness, but when one dwells in an urban environment one has to make do with whatever nature offers. It is about one mile around, just right for Nora and me. It has lovely trees and greenery, and many flowers. In the spring the calla lilies bloom in abundance on the little island that sits in its center. The lake is irregular in shape, so you never see all of it at once (as you do at Walden). But it is nature, and reminds us of whence we come.

Indeed, the lake itself has a long and fascinating history—I have seen pictures of boaters from the nineteenth century, the women wearing dresses with leg o' mutton sleeves and the men clad in dark suits and boater hats. Now you can rent motor boats, or else paddle boats that you propel with your feet. But today, no one is on the lake. Everyone is conscientiously progressing along the sidewalk (each person or group moving along in different directions), but there aren't that many of us here this fall afternoon.

As usual today's other strollers are a mix. Many are elderly. Ancient Chinese fathers are accompanied by dutiful daughters, aging Russian matrons with large bosoms plod stoically ahead with their faded husbands. I hear various languages spoken as well: Spanish, French—almost every part of the world is represented here. Some dialects I don't even recognize. I fit in well with the group, for I am also an elder. I walk faster than some (particularly those on canes), not as fast as others.

There are also a few runners dashing past. This is a good place to run—absolutely flat, not too much foot traffic to slow you down, lots of easy parking nearby. Occasionally a mother wheels her infant past in a baby stroller. There is even a fellow with a backpack and a scraggly beard who looks like he has been on the road a while, but he appears harmless (in the city, you learn to check out every stranger who looks a bit unusual, especially if you yourself are somewhat vulnerable and can't run very fast).

There is also a thin woman who seems to be in hiding—she wears a dark jacket with a hood draped down over her forehead as well as dark glasses. I wonder if she is some celebrity who doesn't want to be recognized (but reflect that her weird garb simply draws attention and curiosity). Again, perhaps she is too sensitive to the sun and has to take care when she is outdoors.

There are ducks and seagulls screaming and circling on the lake, and occasionally Nora makes a dash for them. I have to hold tight to her leash, hoping that she won't pull my shoulder out (the one I have worn a hot pad on for the past two days). Generally, she is well behaved, but once she gets sight (or smell) of some enticing prey, there is almost no stopping her. I shout at her, and jerk her back to the sidewalk. I don't want to lose her. If she breaks away, I could never catch her. She can outrun a greyhound, and has. She settles down and we continue serenely (until the next bird or hidden squirrel).

The light today is special. We approach a knot of slender trees (I never know names) and I notice their glossy surfaces. Next to these lovelies is another, thicker one, with a rumpled veneer. Their beauty manifests as simply "that which is," no fanfare, no display—just themselves the way they are. Somehow I have never noticed these particular trees before. I am almost in mystical awareness—everything is lovely.

Suddenly I realize that I have left my little fanny pack, with my money and credit card, back in the car. We are now halfway round the lake. Should I hurry back? I shrug, decide it is probably safe, and we continue our leisurely stroll.

As we pass the concession stand, I realize that a dog is standing ahead of us, tied to a bench while his "owner" makes a purchase. I wonder if there will be trouble, so I walk Nora up and away from the bench. Then I see the other dog is wagging its tail, and then in fact is thoughtfully involved in scratching its belly with one leg while it balances on the other three. No problem here.

On the final lap, I see more brilliant greens, more ducks to attract Nora's notice, and pass the hooded mystery lady and the "traveler" once again. On the side a tall plant drips with clusters of bell-like purple blossoms. Are they bluebells?

We reach the car. My red pack is safe, though in full view on the front seat.

We stop at the grocery store on our way back. I am thinking how efficiently I am locating all the items on my list, when I realize I can't remember locking the car. Will Nora be safe? They say dogs of this breed fetch a high price, and a city parking lot is more dangerous than the park where we were before.

I pay and check out. I hurry to the car.

Nora is in the back seat, taking a nap. She doesn't even look up as the helper and I load the groceries into the trunk.

We head home, both reassured that there is joy to be had in the world around us.

ALL I HAD

What they appear to want
is a study.
An experiment with
so many of these,
so many of those,
carefully selected and matched,
who knows which was which.

It would of course
need to be replicable.
Otherwise,
how could it be believed
or verified,
readied for review
and publication.

There would have to be
strict controls.
Otherwise,
no one could measure
what happened, nor
how to interpret
the results.

And then I realized,
I could not qualify.
I had nothing to show,
no statistics,
no graphs,

no sheets of repeated
results.

All I had
was what had happened,
the great flash of light
that changed everything
in a single second,
the constantly burning fire,
the afterglow
like an ember
at the bottom of the dish.

DISTANCE HEALING, REIKI, AND THE INTERNET

I have long been fascinated by distance healing—the kind of healing that occurs when the healer and the subject are separated in space, sometimes when they are hundreds (or more) miles apart.

My first experience of this kind of healing occurred several years ago, when the healer and I had set a time for the healing to occur. I felt something stir within a few minutes before the appointed time, and later learned that she had started early.

A friend of mine was once caught in an airport for several hours. She is up in years and was quite uncomfortable sitting on the floor (the only space available) so she called a healer/friend who sent good vibes to her through the airways (or the field, to be more accurate). My friend's discomfort quickly disappeared, and she was able to wait out the delay in peace.

Edgar Mitchell, on the film called "The Divine Matrix" that is being privately circulated, relates his own experience. He was suffering from a kidney problem, so he called a healer hundreds of miles away in Oregon and asked for help. His ailment was soon cured.

All of these stories and more are becoming more and more common. However, I did not realize that similar techniques are now being offered through the Internet. If you go to the following YouTube site, you can experience a group healing from a circle of reiki practitioners. http://www.valleyreiki.com/home

I tried it last night and indeed felt many pleasant sensations as the nine-minute process continued. Of course, I may also have been reacting to the music that accompanies the sessions. And other similar sites are also available on YouTube. I did not find all of these as effective as the Pioneer Valley group.

All of us have healing potential. What if we included such "long distance" transmissions as part of our daily practice? I'm sure that many of us do send prayers to our friends in need, or for the planet itself. Many Buddhists include "all sentient beings" at the conclusion of their prayers.

But what if we did, in fact, regularly send healing energies into the atmosphere? Would the "field" not become stronger and more unified as a result? Would we as a group not benefit?

Even primitive humans used long distance transmission of energies. We know this because certain ancient cave drawings show the male hunters at work, with a line connecting them with their female companions back home. Actually, the line extends from the root of one to the root of the other. The root chakra is a powerful source of energy. And so is the heart. What if we created a vast field of interlinking connections of heart and heart around the world? What then?

part 5

WHAT THE FUTURE HOLDS: THE DIVINE HUMAN

THE STAGES OF SPIRITUAL EVOLUTION

YEARNING

The time of yearning is one of the most important stages in the spiritual journey. It may last months or years, or lifetimes, even. The disciple must want, beyond all else, some sign or token or intimation that there is hope for connection with something yet unseen. It is the ache of the heart for the invisible other, the something more that is sensed but not yet manifest.

CONCLUSION: Always attend to the inner voice. When you are ready, it will speak to you in a distinctive tone, and focus your psyche on what is after all most important—finding your authentic self.

SEEKING

This is the period of active search, through books, teachers, practices which one tries out to see what ensues. One tests and explores. One seeks and either finds or rejects. Often it is during this period that a "false teacher" will arise. If one is victim of such spiritual fraud, one may turn away from the path entirely, or else try other approaches. Now the devotee is a wiser, less vulnerable pilgrim. Innocence has been lost, but a certain protection has been gained.

CONCLUSION: Find the approach that is right for you. You will intuitively recognize it, in the way you discover the right life partner or the perfect vocation. Avoid the "one size fits all" approach.

UNION

Ecstatic union may or may not come in this lifetime. Earnest practice will not guarantee it. Service in the name of a higher power will not ensure that such an epiphany will occur. Grace alone operates in this sphere. Whatever form the revelation takes, it will be a monumental surprise. It may come suddenly, as in the "lightening flash" of awakening. It may be the result of long effort over time. Seeming lack of success in no way means your efforts are in vain, or that you are somehow a less worthy person. There is great benefit for both you and those about you if you are steadfast in your search, for you are "making your soul," as Yeats put it. But now you are entering the world of pure Mystery, and no one can be certain how it will unfold.

CONCLUSION: Love comes to us in many ways, and all are of value.

INTEGRATION

This is one of the last stages (for most of us in this incarnation). We seek to bring together the old and the new beings within, we give ourselves now to one, now to the other. We pursue our chosen practice, and may feel that we have been kissed by the divine. But we also try to reclaim our place in the world, looking perhaps the same as we did before but utterly transfigured within. We try to perform our usual functions in society, with greater or lesser success. We may suddenly reject our old occupations, and even withdraw completely from the world for a time. We long to find others to tell our story to. We are "reborn," but who are we now?

CONCLUSION: This process will continue one way or another for the rest of our lives. We will constantly discover new experience, novel revelation, experience fresh infusions of mystery. We will never know exactly what it is that has occurred, but we will follow with trust and assurance. We cannot name it exactly, but we know that this transformation is why we have been born.

RETURNING THE GIFT

Now our foremost desire is to give back to the world some of the fruits of our journey. We will find ways to share according to our individual talents and capacities. What we want most of all is to help others who are struggling in a similar search. In this way, the benefit becomes universal, not merely personal.

SUMMATION

These are some of the traditional stages of the archetypal journey. It is the most important of all life experiences, for it has to do with the soul's discovery of its true nature and place in the universe. Each person will experience the process in unique terms, for each is truly a being of a special design.

KUNDALINI AND THE INTERNET:
CREATING THE FIELD

Indeed, Kundalini can flow through the Internet, even when you are not expecting it.

This morning, as I read a brief e-mail from a dear friend, I realized that very soft, sweet energy was moving in my hands and forearms. The letter was from someone who is himself very spiritually evolved—he has spent many years of devotion to the ultimate divine, and leads and instructs others in the practice. It was as if his own gentle energies were coming through to me, like a soft salutation.

I think this is how the "Field" will manifest. We will each be centers of energy, sending and receiving these delicate bliss waves from one another as greetings and acknowledgment. And this is why we must keep refining and lifting our own energies—so that when the signals are sent forth, we will be proper receptors. What good is a signal if the receiver is dead?

And in fact the signals are coming in now strong and clear from "other world" sources. Whether these be angels, or presiding spirits, or divine presences of love, or even some as yet unrecognized form of "alien" existence—we sense that some invisible, mysterious, and unknown reality is guiding us on this journey. It is a joint project and, although we do not necessarily see or hear or name these unseen agents, we sense that they are there and that they and we are together "co-creating" a new form of communication and a new way of being.

Yes, gratitude is in order. How blessed we are to be included in this all important process in which humanity itself is moving to a higher stage in its evolutionary journey.

Some have called this progression the "divinization of matter." We ourselves, as bodies made of "water and clay," are the matter that is being transformed in this sacred alchemy by which we return to Source. God throws us out into the world, then reels us back again with threads of love.

UNITING WITH THE GOD

SHIVA'S BRIDEGROOM

(Taken from a description of a sculpture in the San Francisco
Asian Museum: "After the ceremony for his arranged marriage,
the Shaivite poet-saint Sambandar begged Shiva to unite with him
and thus liberate him from all earthly ties. At this word a great
blaze of light enveloped him as he, his bride, and all the guests
entered final union with his god.")

Then he became a flame.
Tendrils of fire played
along his lips, his brow,
his cheeks blossomed in tiny petals of light.

His body shone, like a god
coming to birth.

A sudden crimson flare,
Then nothing remained but a halo of gold,
a bronze shadow gleaming, translucent,
to mark where he had been.

MYTH, TRANSCENDENCE, AND THE SPIRIT OF THE AGE

WHAT IS HAPPENING

Moment to moment
we ask, what is happening?
The sound of shattering everywhere,
is it the world, fragmenting at last,
or our own hearts cracking,
the final break-up of ice?

(from *Some Kiss We Want: Poems Selected and New*)

Ours is one of the most turbulent and the most exciting times in history. Our violence is immense in its scale and its long-term consequences. And, in addition, we have lost the romantic vision. In the past, there was often the aura of the transcendent: the visionary realms of poetry, spiritual beliefs, and other approaches offering meaning and social coherence, suffusing and elevating the familiar human realm. Often even warriors were imbued with a sense of honor and higher purpose—e.g., the codes of honor which supported the warriors in Beowulf, the high vision of divine guidance in The Iliad, one of the bloodiest of all epics. There was real good, real evil—as Dante witnessed and catalogued.

But today many of the myths are exploded, rejected entirely or else reduced to the jingoism and slogans of the masses, cheapened by political exploitation—shams that any thoughtful observer readily rejects. (By myth, I do not mean a falsehood, but rather the universal narratives that connect us all.)

But there is one area where myths survive and are yoked to mystery in their ancient marriage. That is in the still accessible spiritual realm, where experience outruns analysis, and transcendent vision is authenticated by inner alchemy. This is the mythic made real, the archetypes brought to life through crisis and confrontation.

Kundalini itself embodies one of the most ancient and honored of these patterns: the recurrent accounts of gods and humans united in myths and legends of many cultures, for Kundalini permits us to fuse with that unknown reality that we term the divine. This mingling is in fact a sacred marriage, a reenactment of the oft-told story of the god coming down to mate with the merely human. It is, as one person put it, indeed god moving through your body (but only when you are in proper alignment.) It is the state of unconditional love, the taste of heaven on earth.

KUNDALINI AS LOVE-BLISS

This site (www.lovebliss.eu/Kundalini.htm) by Jan Esmann includes a fascinating account of Jan's own ongoing awakening through the years, and meditation exercises to awaken and enhance Kundalini. He refers to Kundalini in the traditional way as a snake that rises up the spine.

I am always interested in those who describe Kundalini as a "snake." Jan even gives the actual dimensions of the snake as he experienced it. My own awakening was quite different, and indeed, this form, though rare, is described in certain of the ancient texts. My energies first awakened in the root/second chakras and then shot almost instantaneously into the crown, which then opened to receive the divine energies from above. I find that each Kundalini opening is unique, and follows its own path. But all may lead (sooner or later) to love-bliss, which itself may be experienced in differing degrees of intensity and feeling.

This author (Esmann), like many others, says that the energies must first reach the heart before reaching the brain, the center where ultimate bliss awakens. Again, my own experience is different from this. At the moment of awakening, the bliss-energies shot into the brain and the opening was indeed one of acute bliss, "like a thousand petals opening." It was some time thereafter that I experienced the true opening of the heart, in an ecstasy that was "almost more than I could bear."

Today (years later) I felt some "love-bliss" during my practice, but it was quite mild in comparison to earlier times. It felt like soft light playing over my arms and face as I moved slowly before my Thangka of Buddha. I was actually "stroking my aura," that is to say, stroking my flesh from about three or four inches away. Was this experience one of Kundalini— or some other form of bliss, such as chi energy moving delicately through? Does it matter? Each experience is different, and each person experiences differently from others.

One thing I especially like about Jan's entry is its explanation of Self-Realization without Shakti (somatic bliss) and Self-Realization with bliss. The former is the state many enter when they feel total loss of self-awareness and become One with the ineffable. No bliss as a feeling state is involved, though the practitioner may describe the experience as "bliss consciousness." In the latter (feeling) state, the bliss itself is the realization of Oneness with Divinity.

Personally, I feel fortunate to be able to enter the love-bliss state in whatever form, for this seems to me to be the ultimate condition of the mortal striving to taste heaven.

THE LOVER

The red gold labia
of the rose,
already beginning to
wither and curl,
how beautiful,
even as death
offers a kiss.

Are You the Friend
or are You the Beloved?
Who cares what name
You bring?
It is only your touch
that matters.

Some call it a tavern,
some a chapel.
God is everywhere.

Take this breast
into your mouth
and drink.
Let your tongue
taste god.

KUNDALINI, TANTRA, AND THE AGING PROCESS

Fine silk rather than rough wool.

Birdsong at dawn,
not the trumpet sounding
before the approaching army.

Delicate as raindrops
falling softly on the branches
of the mountain pine,
not the deluge descending in tumult
to swallow the city.

Light playing,
hovering,
over cheek and brow,
against shoulder and breast.
Illumination within
and without.
Who am I now?

coherence, suffusing and elevating the familiar human realm. Often even warriors were imbued with a sense of honor and higher purpose—e.g., the codes of honor which supported the warriors in Beowulf, the high vision of divine guidance in The Iliad, one of the bloodiest of all epics. There was real good, real evil—as Dante witnessed and catalogued.

But today many of the myths are exploded, rejected entirely or else reduced to the jingoism and slogans of the masses, cheapened by political exploitation—shams that any thoughtful observer readily rejects. (By myth, I do not mean a falsehood, but rather the universal narratives that connect us all.)

But there is one area where myths survive and are yoked to mystery in their ancient marriage. That is in the still accessible spiritual realm, where experience outruns analysis, and transcendent vision is authenticated by

MORE ON KUNDALINI AND THE ELDER

We sometimes wonder how our Kundalini energies will be affected as we age. Will they weaken or disappear? Will we still be able to experience rapture in some form? Will our bodies and nervous systems revert to an earlier state, one in which we moved through the world in "normal," more familiar fashion?

I can only speak from my own experience, since as far as I know no one has looked closely into this subject to discover any common themes.

I now write this at the age of 89, some 36 years after my original awakening. For me the Kundalini process has been a long and sometimes challenging, sometimes rapturous experience. My inner process (I think of this as a form of meditation) has changed constantly over time as I have explored various forms of devotional practice, from movement to deep listening of music to bowing before my Buddhist thangka on my living room wall to reading of sacred poetry and divers sacred texts to listening to Tibetan overtone chanting to other modes I could include.

My basic conclusion is this: Kundalini continues well into age, although it constantly shifts in texture, form, cause, and frequency. It becomes softer, gentler, more subtle. It requires less effort to experience bliss. Instead of the broad movements of hatha yoga, mini movements of the hands or hips suffice. One learns to experience the sweet energies of the aura itself just by moving the hands in circles a few inches from the body. These delicate, ethereal sensations confirm our sense of divine connection as much as did the intense and thrilling raptures of the beginning. What was in the early stages like a brass band marching through our living room is now like the sound of a soft flute playing in the distance, but they are equally delightful.

We no longer need to "practice" in a regular fashion, since the Beloved Within often visits in surprise moments. We may wake up already feeling bliss stirring in our hands and arms or elsewhere. We may be taken into unexpected ecstasy by listening to sacred music as we sit in front of our computers listening to the Internet. Sometimes it begins with inhaling the scent of essential oils, particularly when these include frankincense. We often mirror in our own bodies the lovely energies emanating from certain chakras of friends or others standing before us. Holding special crystals can awaken bliss within. When we stand in front of certain paintings or other works of art, we may "pick up" the creator's own energies, embedded in the image and now emanating from it as universal love/bliss. Likewise, when we visit certain sacred locations (I think of Ireland here) we may feel the earth energies rise up through our bodies and carry us into rapture.

We no longer experience the disruptive "ups and downs" of the early stages when our bodies sought to integrate new and unfamiliar frequencies.

We experience deep peace within ourselves, and find it easier to maintain calm in the face of crisis.

Our focus turns from our own demanding inner process to helping others as best we can to understand and survive the profound transformation now happening to them and countless numbers across the globe as we together move through planetary initiation. We strive to send our energies out into the universe to help and heal those facing health and other challenges.

We continue to feel gratitude that we are included in this vast and enigmatic process, orchestrated elsewhere and enfolding us in Love from the Divine Source of all Love that is.

KUNDALINI AND THE ELDER, CONTINUED

When I was younger, I said it was difficult to distinguish between the symptoms of Kundalini and menopause. Now I say much the same about Kundalini and the aging process. Who knows which is which? Am I younger or older in my body because of the Kundalini experience? Is it more or is it less difficult to sustain the energies? Have I harmed or helped myself by my prolonged experience? Would I be better off—able to make a more effective gift to others—if I were now 40 (or 50 or even 60)?

What will people think when they see me, with all the attributes and manifest imperfections of age? What will they make of the fact that my physical energies are limited, and other difficulties are apparent (stiffness, slowed movement, etc.)?

I am not a perfect specimen, either from the standpoint of health or appearance. I look like an ordinary woman, with ordinary features for a person at my age (now in my eighties). So—where does all this lead?

The psychic who did a brilliant phone reading for me several years ago spoke to this concern in that early session. He said people would be willing to listen to me because no one—absolutely no one—was less pretentious, less intimidating. That part seems to be quite right.

The bottom line: I must, like anyone else my age, do whatever I can to "sustain the vessel," to maintain good health and well being in order to fulfill the rest of this curious destiny, which I have chosen, or which has chosen me.

I think I have reached the age when I am more ready to take a risk. Why not?

AN AUDIENCE THAT UNDERSTANDS

Recently, I visited a class in a nearby university that is dedicated to spiritual growth and transcendence. I spoke on "Rumi as Poetic Inspiration" and read some of my poems which were inspired by or were responses to Rumi. I also described my spiritual practice (at present mainly deep listening to sacred music, with some slow movement included.)

I was gratified that the classes were extremely responsive. They understood that my "journey"—though not the same as theirs—and my "practice" both gave them permission to follow their own paths, whatever those might be. One said she loved the energy path, but had been made to feel that she should do quiet sitting as "real meditation." Another woman said that as I read from Unmasking the Rose she could see my face in the rose on the cover. Then she began to sob, lamenting that she too wanted a lover (I don't know if she meant human or divine). I held her in my arms for several minutes—clearly this was what she longed for.

My journey now consists to a great extent of sharing with others, and supporting them on their own journeys. I have kept up a heavy correspondence with an interesting "Kundalini initiate" who lives on an organic farm in Washington state and can bring up the energies whenever she chooses by placing her tongue on the roof of her mouth. It seems that this has become a pattern for me—to discover a new friend and then to explore the relationship in some depth via e-mail. The Internet makes for a delightful way to meet new friends with similar (spiritual) interests. Indeed, Brian the psychic was right: he told me I was going to emerge from isolation and meet "many new and wonderful friends."

This time of connection was prophesied to me very many years ago after my initial opening, during the fifteen years I spent in spiritual isolation with no real friends or comrades on a similar path. Because I was so alone on my journey for so long, each new friend is very precious, for the time of moving ahead together has come.

The circles are closing—the networks are forming at an ever-increasing rate, on many levels of consciousness.

GROUP ENERGIES AND SHOWING UP

In the class I mentioned earlier, the teacher performed some rituals, such as prostrating himself at my feet, and having the class surround me and send loving energies. I was embarrassed by all this adulation, and then I was informed that I was the center of attention because I had been chosen to represent the goddess. Everything was charged, as if we all entered an energy field together, a field of vital love and sensuous feeling, a preview of the future, perhaps. I think of this state as "group spirit," the sharing and intensifying of energies through common realization.

After this and subsequent activities, I was totally exhausted for the next week. When I finally felt a bit more normal, I played the "Trance Tara" tape of Jonathan Goldman (I had been playing it off and on for several days) and had what I could only call "Supreme Ecstasy." All I can say is that it literally went beyond all other experiences, so much so that I had to quit after only 15 minutes, and lie down. But, of course, I felt terrible the next day, and actually thought I would not want to continue this process if the price continued to be so high. So I vowed, "Eschew ecstasy...walk more in the park, and eat more strawberries."

In other words, follow a middle path between extremes, and enjoy a more "normal" state of being. But of course after a few days, I succumbed once more to temptation, listened to the same piece, and again felt engulfed in exquisite bliss waves—intense but not at quite the same level as before. And since then, I have repeated the experience, always with the same tape, and walking afterward when I could.

Today I started out feeling great, energized and well balanced. I did my laundry, carrying the basket back and forth across the street to the laundromat at the corner. Then I decided to try the Trance Tara tape again, but it didn't feel right. I had a few pleasant sensations, but nothing like previous sessions. And I even felt a bit nauseous, so I quit after some 20 minutes. It is as if something else decided.

I cannot make the raptures happen. I can simply "show up" and be ready in case "they" decided to manifest. Again, I am groping my way forward, not knowing exactly what or how to approach the experience, hoping that I am doing the right thing.

ANGELS AND SOUL GROUPS

This morning, as I was doing my morning meditation (standing, doing slight movements with my arms, all in front of my Buddhist thangka) I had an inner "vision." Before I started I had looked briefly at Ajit Mookerjee's beautiful book called Kundalini: The Arousal of the Inner Energies, with its fascinating illustrations, for I knew that even glancing at such potent images could arouse my own bliss feelings. Then I began more or less to "daydream" about another way to increase the energies. I was thinking of my women's writing circle—we seem to share much in common as to our life paths and our spiritual natures. Indeed, we seem to be a "soul group." As I pondered this notion, an image floated in—I imagined that one of the group was standing directly behind me (say, two feet away) and the other three were lined up behind her, all of us experiencing sweet flowing bliss, currents that moved through one to another. Our formation thus was a geometric image, with one person at the head and the others lined up behind.

Soul groups are often thought of as small groups of like-minded spirits who are drawn together in the "interims" to form a collective consciousness and shared energy field. (And you can belong to more than one such group.) What I was viewing in my inner vision was such a collective, almost as if we were practicing for some later stage when we would again participate in a similar group consciousness.

And then it came to me—what if angels (who often come in groups, rather than alone) themselves were arranged in geometric patterns—triangles or squares or even spirals of energy—and thus their own energies were strengthened through their shared field? And—of course—the arrangement could vary (in the way that birds in flight sometimes shift the pattern of the formation).

And, finally, this notion reminded me of the curious behavior of the various unidentified objects so often described as moving in seemingly random, shifting patterns, which we often discern as lights blinking about their edges. Perhaps the UFOs are angels in disguise, dematerialized energy fields, moving through our "space," for purposes that are not clear.

What would happen if we too created such shared energy fields now, on this plane, while we are still on planet earth? I think our power to heal and bless might surprise us.

ARE WE AFRAID TO AWAKEN?

Imagine a camera, the old fashioned kind with two images you have to bring into alignment in order to get a proper focus. These two images, seeking to unite, represent the being you think you are and the being that is your true self. Only when the two are one, will you transcend the polarities and awaken to the knowledge of your own essential nature. This state is called Enlightenment.

We have heard these words many times from various teachers. They tell us to let go, release all petty concerns of the personal level, the irrelevant issues and hang ups that prevent us from proper realization.

Yet we cling. We hold on desperately to what we think of as our identity— that persona which society and our own choices have created as our "being vehicle."

What holds us back from the leap of faith demanded to enter the longed for state? Why do we not release our ties to samsara, the "unreal" world of material existence, and enter the transcendent realm of the realized ones?

It is above all fear that holds us back. Fear of losing those things which most define us in the everyday world—our professional identities, our family and social roles, friendships, our entanglements on all levels. Even our failures and unresolved conflicts help to tell us who we are. And, in our innermost being, we hold them tightly, for without them, we lack definition and thus may become nothing.

To make the transit to the next level, where the small and greater are fused, we must release our tight grip on the false image, letting it flow into the ether, and in the state of perfect openness, accept the infusion of something unknown, yet uncannily familiar. We must be willing to remove the barriers, if necessary tear down the doors, and let in the god waiting outside. Only then will our fears fall away, our obsessive cravings shrink, and our true nature be revealed as beings of limitless wisdom, compassion, and love.

At this point, we do not leave the world, but become more fully in it, able to walk freely, offering gifts of service and beauty, secure in our newfound knowledge—that to become no one is to become all things and everyone.

REFLECTIONS ON ENLIGHTENMENT

I am going to be very bold in this reflection, for I am going to speak from the perspective of the enlightened being. It may seem (indeed is) strange, even a mark of extreme hubris, to assume such authority. Yet, for the moment, this is what I propose.

I make no claim to be enlightened, but I think I have in fact had a taste of this wondrous state, and that provides a starting place. I also draw upon whatever I may have gained from having lived in this world and both experienced and witnessed it in its many manifestations for over eight decades.

I use the question and answer format, touching on issues which concern all of us who pursue this topic.

Anything I say is, of course, personal speculation, based on private intuition and inner reflection. It is a foray into the mysterious, an experiment in exploration of the unknown, and hence fully subject to revision and restatement.

Q. Why does enlightenment take many lifetimes? Why can't we simply leap to that peak of knowing quickly, effortlessly, in the present moment?

A. Enlightenment involves the complete evolution of the entire being. All levels must be dealt with—emotional, psychological, mental, physical, as well as spiritual. All emotional issues must be resolved, whether major or minor. Abuse feelings must be healed, ego inflation and self-rejections likewise brought into balance. Such full self-understanding, correction, and acceptance can occur only over many lifetimes of immersion in the world, in a variety of circumstance, and diverse milieus. One travels the razor's edge, where one shifts too far now this way, now that, seeking a balance that seems eternally elusive.

Q. Why do so many encounter extremes in their incarnations—horrific suffering of self or loved ones, or else seemingly unmerited wealth and ease of circumstance?

A. Extremes of suffering are not necessarily karmic retribution for past misdeeds, nor something bargained for ahead of time. They often seem unjustifiable within the framework of a benevolent universe. But they do serve a purpose. That purpose or result is to yield insight into circumstances well beyond the "norms," the safe parameters of ordinary existence. One who has suffered deeply is significantly more able to empathize with the pain and sufferings of others. This in itself is an important advance toward enlightenment. This is true compassion—to know at the heart level what is happening to the victim, the patient, the innocent captive of circumstance and not turn away.

Such extremes of painful experience do indeed carry us more swiftly toward the final goal, and some may actually choose this path before birth to speed the process of spiritual development during incarnation. These too are fully deserving of sympathy and help for the pain they endure is real.

As for those born to a life of ease, if they remain in their comfortable niches, and never sally forth to face the challenges or ordinary life, they forfeit their chances for progress in this lifetime, and prolong their overall process of spiritual evolution.

Q. What does it mean to say someone has had a "taste of enlightenment?"

A. It means that the person has had a glimpse, has entered temporarily into an awareness that all things are but minute parts of a dynamic whole, and that individual identity itself is an illusion, since nothing exists apart from the cosmic reality. We can never know the latter in its fullness, for that would kill us—we dare not look god directly in the face, even in moments of high transcendence. But we can experience this divine presence in exquisite moments of stepped down expression—small bits and fragments of the totality itself.

However, no one can live permanently in that exalted (yet diminished) state on earth unless he/she breaks all ties with common reality as we know it. The world of practical affairs and the planes of transcendent truth are not compatible, though they do impinge on one another and occasionally interfuse to some extent.

Further, at this time particularly, there is great need for persons willing to act for the benefit of society at large, and forgo desires for personal enlightenment. Service itself becomes their vehicle for progress. They are the true bodhisattvas, who put the needs of others ahead of private goals.

Q. Must one sever all personal connections (as with lover, family, friends) to enter such advanced states?

A. At some point, one should experience these relationships, with all their complexity and frustrations, in order to encounter and transcend the emotional toll they exact. One must experience them in order to go on. One must not prematurely reject such human experiences, for then the feelings themselves become frozen, and the person is like an icicle frozen in the snow. The point is to open to such experiences, savor their fruits, and then go on to other levels, either in this or another lifetime.

Q. How does one know whether one is progressing or nearing the goal?

A. As one moves forward, the center of personal gravity shifts—one is less absorbed on the ego fixated, personal level, and more attuned to the needs of others, whether large groups or individuals. One seeks not to take from this world, but to discover what one has to give.

Q. What is the role of ecstasy in all of this?

A. Ecstasy is one of the final tests. It, too, must be received with joy and enthusiasm. However, the more susceptible one is to rapture, the more open one is to pain. They may follow one another in swift succession, often in intense manifestation. Again, the purpose is to bring the self into balance, to endure one or the other without being overwhelmed, to maintain balance and equanimity even in the grips of extremes.

Q. If one achieves enlightenment, what purpose will have been served?

A. One will have returned to or joined with one's true nature. One will have come home and know at last who one truly is. One's final longing will then be fulfilled.

ON INNER GUIDES

Dear Friend,

Recently, you wrote to me on e-mail asking for my thoughts on a question pertaining to both outer and inner guidance. Unfortunately, when I attempted to respond, my computer deleted your message before I captured even your e-mail address. Your question was quite thought provoking, and I am writing a partial response here, in the hopes you will see it and that you will write again.

As I recall, you asked about the wisdom of relying on "inner" guides, such as (I am interpolating here) spirit guides, or the spirits of departed saints, or perhaps angelic beings, gods and goddesses and deities of various types. (These are not the terms you used, but various practitioners do rely on such immaterial beings to lead them on their spiritual quest.)

Now, I cannot speak for others, but can only share my own experiences in this realm. Earlier in my life, I was deeply inspired by symbols of the great goddess herself, as depicted in Western culture. For some time, I felt a deep connection with her (like many women of recent times), but ultimately her "felt presence" seemed to grow less vital, and I moved on.

About this same time, I seemed to connect with a true "spirit guide," but broke the connection when something seemed not right about the relationship.

Then, when my major "awakening" occurred, it sprang from deliberate visualization of the god/goddess (Shiva/Shakti) in union, as depicted in an illustration in a book. This meditation is an ancient Tantric practice, and has been used for centuries to awaken the inner energies. (I did not know this at the time. I was a total novice.)

However, after my early efforts, I soon moved on to other choices. For a time I visualized Shiva, then Krishna, and the latter seemed to provide a less intense, more manageable arousal of the energies. Ultimately, I left all images behind, and now focus on the energies themselves, often as "currents of bliss," derived from the universal life source; I then dedicate the entire experience to the healing and transformation of the world and all its life forms. In other words, ecstasy and compassion are joined. (When no ecstasy comes, then compassion is always available.)

Kundalini herself is for many the "the ultimate goddess." For me, she represents the energetic force which lies behind and beyond all the symbols and representations of the goddess, both East and West. Kundalini seems to possess a palpable intelligence, which directs the awakening process as it unfolds, now urging forward, now holding back. When she makes her presence known, I feel in touch with a living presence, which I most frequently think of as "the Beloved Within."

However, this still does not answer your question directly. Again, I can speak only from my own experience. For me, the bottom line is that I do feel in touch with what I can only call a "divine presence." This presence is not particularized by name or form, but is rather sensed indirectly, felt rather than perceived. We do not "converse," in a usual way, although occasionally I do direct specific questions and even solicit help on particular issues. I sometimes characterize this "wisdom voice" as the "inner guru," but I give it no further distinction, other than as my own inner guide, leading me gently and unobtrusively on the right path for me. This inner guru is always there, often in silence, yet available when needed. This unseen consciousness seemed to lead me through the Kundalini process through the years when I had no outer guide. At times the journey was quite difficult, but ultimately I survived.

As I sort out my thoughts, I realize that my "inner guide" has more than one face, just as we as conscious beings do. Sometimes "she" appears as bliss, sometimes as thoughtful observation, sometimes as creative source for poetry. In all of these manifestations, she is leading me ahead to new levels of discovery. Perhaps she is my own "higher self," perhaps more than that. I bow to her before practice, and I feel that she in turn bows back—that I am essential to her own expression, just as she is essential to mine.

I think each of us has such an inner guide, who waits until we are ready to reveal the next stage of our path. I think the common saying, "When the student is ready, the guru will appear," refers to this inner guide, which to some degree is our own innate wisdom and fullness discovered more completely.

For the most part, my contact comes through devotional practice—which often consists of listening to sacred music or poetry, or performing ritual movement, including mudras or bodily poses. At these times, it sometimes happens that I sense the energy body open with a special delight which includes a feeling of being entered or filled with something invisible but indeed wonderful. It is a sense of total love, total acceptance, total fulfillment. It is, in one person's words, as if "god is moving through your body."

As for advice, I think I would say this: The dedication to the divine that manifests without name or form usually arises late in one's spiritual journey. (At least, this is what I have been told.) Before that, one yearns for some more tangible guide, something to give needed direction and encouragement. The danger of focusing on an "inner guide," I would suppose, is that one might end up simply "speaking to oneself" without knowing it, that the "higher being" is in fact merely a projection of one's own imagination. However, if the advice offered is sound and the approach pure, then perhaps the connection is useful. After all, who is to say where the "smaller self" and the "higher self" begin and end?

I guess my final word is, choose the approach that seems right for you. Test your choice against your feelings—are you comfortable with this relationship? Does it seem to lead in the direction you wish to go? Do you feel that this is a connection with beneficial results, opening you to new levels of awareness? If it makes you uncomfortable, if it creates anxiety or makes you uneasy, then I would say, "drop it," no matter what the seeming benefits are. It is easy to get off track with "inner guides," just as certain outer guides may mislead one.

I hope I have presented your question with reasonable accuracy, and that my answer is helpful. Thank you for writing, and for raising this intriguing issue.

Recently, I attended a spiritually focused workshop at a nearby retreat center. I enjoyed the people who came, many of whom were obviously sincere, dedicated people, looking for ways to deepen and expand their spiritual commitments. But the topic of Kundalini was not included (nor did I expect it to be). I even had an energy balancing from a lovely 80-year-old nun, and the experience was quite nice, but she herself seemed to know nothing about Kundalini.

Once again, I felt a bit of the "outsider," the person whose spiritual experience is so out of the ordinary that it seems futile even to bring it up. Most of the meals took place in silence, so I was not able to talk with many there. But on the last day the prohibition was lifted, and during the final lunch, a woman in her thirties sat down next to me at the table and we began to talk. I discovered that she was, like me, a writer, and, when she asked me what I wrote, I told her (after a moment of hesitation) about Unmasking the Rose, my personal spiritual autobiography. Immediately, her expression changed to one of wonder. "I knew there was a reason I sat by you!" she exclaimed.

Then she described for me her own spontaneous Kundalini awakening of a few years back, an experience with many striking parallels with my own. During her awakening, she also went into what I think of as "mystical consciousness," the time when all the world and its beings are suffused with great beauty and love. So, we exchanged key information about our lives and our awakening process in a space of some forty minutes or so, but we each recognized a deep bond with the other.

Such meetings are, I think, highly significant. Each of us learns that we are not alone, that others are also undergoing a similar process, and indeed such radical experiences are occurring worldwide. This in itself is a source of great hope and inspiration for me.

Who knows how far this incredible phenomenon will spread? And who can predict what its consequences will be? Things that start small often grow to mammoth proportions (consider the beginnings and spread of such movements as civil rights, feminism, gay rights, to name a few). No matter how disturbing the events reported in the daily news, another, deeper, and more significant transformation is taking place, beneath the radar of the common press, invisible to many except those who have eyes to see, and ears to hear. There is indeed a "wild card" in the deck, and although we can't name it, it may be the means of our salvation.

An article in today's newspaper highlighted a thought-provoking quote from a contemporary writer: "What passes for optimism is most often the effect of an intellectual error."

This assertion led me to reflect a bit on whether it is possible, even appropriate, to hold on to optimism in the current world of multiple disasters. We seem to be surrounded by crises and threats on all levels. Our faith in human goodness and powers of regeneration is being severely tested. Do we dare to maintain our hope that transcendence is possible in current circumstances?

I like to think that we pass through three major phases in our progress to intellectual and spiritual maturity. The first is that of youthful idealism, the time when one believes that anything is possible, that slogans such as "make love not war" will save the world, and that every change is a sign of progress. Later, disillusionment sets in. We see that persons in authority are often inadequate or corrupt, that many in society are motivated by greed, not innate goodness, and that the bottom line apparently rules in all circumstances. Our intellect confirms such observations with myriad instances. Indeed, it is essential to see through the shams and slogans, to shatter the false myths by which much of society operates. At this point, many become bitter and even cynical, and renounce all hope for a better future.

In order to get beyond this limiting and ultimately self-defeating view, one has to cross a threshold, where mind alone does not rule. True, mind is utterly essential in the restricted realm of "practical" human affairs. It affords protection from charlatans, opens our eyes to deceit and deception, keeps us from falling into all sorts of follies. It also allows for impressive progress on the advance toward understanding of ourselves and our universe.

But mind has set limitations. At some point, those who rely solely on mental approaches are like blind men stumbling against an invisible wall. Their progress is halted, for at this point they are relying on the wrong instruments to see.

There is a universe outside the apparent realm of familiar experience. To enter, we must be willing to open on a new level, to take immeasurable risk, to voyage into uncharted space. Here are the spheres of the transcendent, the places unmarked on any atlas and unnamed on any map of the universe. To find them, we must risk all in what T. S. Eliot calls "the awful daring of a moment's surrender." "Only then will we find 'it'," the treasure locked within, the Self we have yearned for so long.

We will not be hopelessly blinded by our new vision. We will continue to acknowledge the shadow as well as the redeeming light. Glory and horror, suffering and transcendence—all will be recognized as realities existing together in our limited human plane.

Kundalini operates to awaken us to the possibilities of transcendence. Once this light flows through us, we know through the testimony of our own bodies and spirits that redemption can come in unsuspected ways and transformation may occur in surprising circumstances. Such transfiguration becomes the ground for perpetual affirmation, the basis for undying hope, for now we have entered "the still point of the turning world." (Eliot)

Transcendence is no longer a concept to be proved, but a reality to be experienced in common sense practices. And this is the time to deal with all unresolved psychological issues, the hang ups left over from childhood as well as those that arise from the present. Kundalini has been described as the "rotor-rooter of the soul," and any unresolved problems will present themselves dramatically during the awakening process.

Many tapes of sanskrit chanting or sacred music from various traditions are available. One should, I think, seek that which will elevate and not degrade the self, whether in reading or media or friends or close relationships.

And it goes without saying that compassionate action, generous sharing, dedication to the welfare of earth and all its beings is paramount. What would be the value of a bliss which did not include concern for others as well as self?

When I look at this list, it sounds a bit like preaching. I think the truth is one does not so much "seek" certain kinds of experience, as simply be drawn to them, naturally and effortlessly, for they perform like spiritual magnets, drawing the spirit forward. Each will choose her own path, each select her own form of progression, whether from books or association with others, or music, or movement, or service or creative activity, or whatever. "There are many ways of approaching the throne." You will know what is "right" for you. As Campbell says, "Follow your bliss," and thus (I think) you prepare for transcendence, with many "illuminating moments" along the way.

And—it seems that the morphogenetic field of Kundalini is growing, thus permitting more and more to awaken, with greater ease and in ever increasing numbers. "Like is drawn to like."

One of the frustrations for those of us who have undergone the experience is (often) not being able to give the gift to others. But who knows, perhaps each one of us is giving something of value all the time, just by our actions and loving presence.

In the Sufi tradition, yearning itself is an important initial stage of the spiritual journey. By yearning for the divine, one inevitably is drawn closer to that unseen presence, and many believe that the divine also yearns for us.

For years, my Texas friend and I have kept in touch through e-mail and telephone conversations, sharing our spiritual and creative journeys and offering support to one another. We have each been grateful to have some other person to tell when unusual or even bizarre Kundalini phenomena occurred, for these are often not the sort of happenings you would want to reveal to just anyone.

A few years ago, when her husband retired, they moved to a rural area near a major city. Oh my, I thought, she will never meet anyone there who will understand her Kundalini journey, or who has even have heard of the subject of Kundalini.

How wrong I was. She has found, in this basically out-of-the-way place, several kindred souls. In fact, she discovered two others who are also dealing with radical Kundalini transformation (one an acupuncturist and the other an energy worker). The three now meet regularly to meditate together in a simple but profound way. They merely hold hands and let the sweet energies circulate among them. My friend says it is one of the deepest and richest experiences she has had, and suggests that in our current stage of evolution, we are forming groups with similar travelers to enhance our mutual progress.

I think she is right. About twenty years ago, when I was living in near total spiritual isolation, I wrote in my journal (in a kind of channeled entry) that at first, the journey for each awakening one would be extremely lonely, for we would have few or no companions to accompany us along the way. But, as time progressed, more and more of us would experience Kundalini awakening, and ultimately the phenomenon would spread rapidly to critical mass and the leap to the new stage of evolution.

As my friend commented, Kundalini now seems to be occurring virtually everywhere, even in such unlikely places as small towns in Texas.

Today, Kundalini yoga centers seem to be found on virtually every corner (at least where I live), and people eagerly enroll in workshops and webinars that once were considered esoteric spiritual topics.

When I moved to Boulder some eight years ago, I knew almost no one who shared my spiritual interests. Now I seem to bump into such people wherever I go—in the grocery store, at the dentist's office, at the dermatologist's office, sometimes sitting next to me at concerts. Often they are familiar with Kundalini, and share as well my interest in such spiritual writers as Rumi, Hafiz, and Kabir. Through the Internet, I am now in touch with others here and over the world. At first, I was hesitant to speak openly of my experience and hence spent some fifteen years in silence and isolation. Now I do a blog on Kundalini (the source of these entries) as well as a Facebook page.

And, my early journal entry also foresaw the creation of "soul groups," spirits connected in fundamental ways, even though each participant retained a separate identity. And such bands are forming here and there, in various ways, as if some guiding intelligence were orchestrating the entire event.

Recently, I met with a group of women to organize our own women's spirituality circle. We began with a twenty-minute silent meditation. Usually, I get little out of this kind of meditation, and often sit more or less fidgeting and wondering how soon the session will be over. My subtle energies retreat in shyness, unwilling to manifest in such an unprotected setting.

This time, something unexpected occurred. For the first time ever in such a setting, the bliss energies stirred and then bloomed into full ecstasy as we sat in silent communion. I realized that something quite special had happened. For me it was a breakthrough experience, as if my bliss body had finally lost its shyness and was ready at last to "come out" in public.

Whatever is going on, my friend and I agree that we feel extremely blessed to be part of the process as it proceeds toward its own destined end.

KUNDALINI AND HUMAN EVOLUTION

Is Kundalini the primary agent for the evolution of humanity to a new level of consciousness?

Before attempting to answer such a profound question, we must first step back, think a bit about the implications, and introduce some qualifiers. By looking at the issue from various angles, we may be able to unveil the knowledge we are seeking.

Aren't there other paths to expansion of consciousness, perhaps to enlightenment itself?

Yes, there are many paths to higher awareness, to spiritual growth, and to transcendent states of being. All are valid, all are rich sources of inner development, all contribute immeasurably to the benefit of humankind. But Kundalini offers something more, an additional factor that completes the mix and lifts the self to a stage of being not available through other approaches.

How does the Kundalini state differ from more familiar "mystical consciousness?" Mystics of all ages report being infused with a sense of divine love, of sensing their own oneness with all that is, and of perceiving the unending beauty of the world which surrounds them.

Kundalini can trigger such states of mystical awareness, and these are for all purposes the same as those reported by the mystics of many traditions. Kundalini thus can include mystical awareness but it embraces more.

How is Kundalini consciousness different from the kinds of expanded awareness reported worldwide, such as ESP, auras, telepathic communication, precognition, energy healing, sensing sacred earth centers, remote viewing?

Again, Kundalini can include some of these capacities as part of the renewal process, but it involves a great deal more. (Some people think such abilities are themselves valid expressions of Kundalini manifestation.)

What is the "something more" which a Kundalini experience provides?

When Kundalini manifests most fully, the crown opens and the Immensity flows in. This is an indescribably ecstatic moment, where the brain itself seems to be flooded with bliss. The sense of self surrenders to an awareness of a vaster, more comprehensive reality. The ego then confronts its own non-existence, and realizes that its sense of separate identity is a fiction, and that it exists only as a minute atom in an infinitely large pulsating web of being. This reality cannot be adequately described, but it can be experienced as infinite divine love, which holds the human in its ecstatic embrace. From this point on, the Lover Within becomes a familiar feature of daily experience, something quite real, not a mere metaphor.

Kundalini now infuses every pore, every thought, every deep memory and held emotion of the initiate. What follows is a thorough inner cleansing, which may go on for months or years, as the human is remade physically and spiritually. Sometimes the reshaping process involves painful readjustment of the psyche and body as the self undergoes deep alchemical transformation.

Is the initiate now in a state of enlightenment?

Perhaps there are a few such examples of saints and others who have reached this exalted state as a permanent condition. The vast majority of us experience significant progress on our inner journeys, arriving at a more advanced level, but not that of full enlightenment. The evolutionary shift does not occur all at once for the individual initiate nor for the group. It is an ongoing event, occurring at various speeds and manifesting in various ways.

Why can't one simply accept this realization intellectually (that we are all part of something greater) without undergoing such a demanding process?

Evolution is a tremendous undertaking. It is more than mind. It is soul in the fullest sense. One must experience it at the cellular level of body and in the deepest reaches of spirit for it to achieve its aims.

What are the other benefits of the process? Are people better, wiser, more compassionate and loving? Are all their personal problems solved and do their lives become one unending experience of bliss?

Once one is filled with such evidence of a divine reality that holds humankind in its embrace, it is all but impossible to return to earlier states of disillusionment or despair. One knows in the most convincing way that supreme love and power are real, that divine presence is not an untested theory, but a truth which plays out daily in one's life.

What one does with this immeasurable gift varies with one's own interests and abilities. We are surrounded by people dedicating themselves to helping humankind reach this new level, many working with little concern for personal gain. They become healers, poets, teachers, and helpers of various kinds, committed to "bringing the treasure back home."

Are all Kundalini experiences of the type described above?

No. Many Kundalini manifestations (such as intense heat or cold or muscle spasms) are symptomatic of the beginning stages. Sometimes the "awakening" is temporary, and disappears after the early episodes. Sometimes it disappears for long periods, years even, and then unexpectedly returns.

Why are we hearing so much about Kundalini now, when it was almost unknown only a few years ago?

We are creating what Rupert Sheldrake called a "morphogenetic field." Once the phenomenon is established, it occurs more and more frequently, and will become ever more prevalent as time passes. At critical mass, it will become the prevailing form of consciousness.

How do people who have undergone a significant portion of this process recognize each other?

Often through the vibratory level. They sense (in a palpable fashion) the energies of the other person, and often feel these as bliss or resonance in their own subtle bodies. (But not every person with beautiful energies has consciously undergone the Kundalini transformation process, and vice versa.)

Sometimes they discover that they have common interests in the area of spiritual transformation, especially as that involves Kundalini awakening. Often they are delighted to connect with such "spiritual buddies" with whom they can speak openly about their own experiences. As one initiate said, "It is the only game in town."

Once one has had such a taste of fuller awareness, nothing remains the same. The moment of awakening is the "moment that changes everything."

Kundalini restructures the nervous system itself. Therefore one hears with new ears, sees with new eyes, and feels with new impulses. In its ultimate and ideal expression, life becomes infused with wonder and delight. We feel at a more basic, essential level. And, because we (as a species) are already so highly developed in our left brain spheres of operation, we can fuse the disparates more fully, logic and intuition, reason and ecstasy, intellect and delight.

MORE ON KUNDALINI AND EVOLUTION

Evolution as a general concept typically refers to physical evolution (Darwin) or else mental development (brain function). The next stage (as Teilhard affirmed) will be spiritual evolution, a new way of being in the universe. Kundalini is, I believe, the mechanism by which this new state will be attained.

Of course, there have always been persons among us who were highly "spiritually evolved." Certain saints and seekers of all times and places have sometimes reached impressive heights in their spiritual development.

But frequently these "high achievers" in the spiritual realms have discounted or ignored the body (including the energetic body) in their efforts toward holiness. Indeed, often the central purpose of their exertions has been to transcend or overcome all physical or emotional needs.

Now, a problem arises here when we speak of the "body." There is the material body (often condemned for its "impurities") and the energetic body, sometimes called the body of light. This radiant shell encloses and enfolds the other, more substantial self. They exist in tandem, and are a close knit unit, yet many are unaware of the light body's very existence.

Kundalini acts as a switch or trigger to awaken the light body and bring it into consciousness. For the first time, one realizes that there is a way of knowing, of comprehending, of feeling which goes well beyond the limits of the five senses. Accepted concepts, familiar world views crumble or explode before the new revelation. One opens to the embrace of the divine in an unimaginable way. It is as if all one's atoms and cells are suddenly lit up, bringing ecstatic bliss of union to every particle of the being. The atom of self is flung into a new orbit, the ultimate quantum leap.

One realizes that he/she has been living in half a world, or perhaps a world of half-truth. That what one previously accepted as "reality" was fundamentally skewed, that there are ways of feeling, of being, of connecting far beyond what anyone had dreamed. Now consciousness is more than mental activity (though one does not abandon mind). Awareness is extended, as if an unsuspected door had swung open to reveal a "secret garden" within.

One senses at a deeper level. One feels both pain and pleasure as these originate at the cellular level. What before was coarse perception is now subtle, what was previously unknown now becomes one's habitual mode.

And the hallmark of the experience is bliss. Bliss comes not as a one night visitor, but a familiar beloved who arrives again and again, perhaps stirred by music, perhaps by the beauty of a natural setting, perhaps by the presence of a similarly awakened one. A sacred text, a mantra, a gathering of the devout—all can trigger the inner currents of joy.

And because one has opened so fully to love, one now loves in a new way. Everything one sees or encounters reveals its unique beauty, each face is like a variant of one's own. Of course, one feels renewed compassion for all that is, for one now perceives that the seeming external is in fact merely an aspect of one's own self. There is one world soul, one world being, and all are participants in its ongoing creative unfoldment.

This, I think, is the basis for the next stage of evolution—to know that "god" (goddess), the divine, the sacred, the immensity—is available as deeply felt personal presence. To realize that although our familiar notions of self are based on fantasy, we and all that exists are connected in a most fundamental fashion as integral atoms of the vast indefinable real.

And this, I believe, is enlightenment—to know this reality of being as a lived experience, not merely something to be posited or discussed or arrived at through logic.

There are many stations on the way up the mountain. All are beautiful and all are significant. But there is a difference between those who know the mountain is there, and have experienced its intimate nature in "new consciousness" and those who remain oblivious to such vision, laboring still with the tools and perspectives of "old consciousness."

It is difficult and indeed perhaps not possible to persuade those who have yet to experience the "new awareness" that it exists as a reality and not a phantasm. But once one undergoes such transmutation, one lives in constant wonder and delight at the blessings it bestows.

Such is the nature of the completed journey. As for the present, we are in the transition time, and few live stabilized in the final vision or goal. Many of us continue to labor, often swinging between the extremes of bliss and pain, transcendence and despair, conviction and uncertainty. The reordering of humanity is a difficult process, but transmutation does occur. The process is a demanding one, as if a determined alchemist tried again and again to find the right formula to transmute the base metals of the ordinary mortal into the gold of the sublime.

Some today are speaking of actual mutation of the human species, in the way that the caterpillar becomes a butterfly or a fish turns into a bird.

SECRET PLEASURES, PRIVATE GRIEFS

For years, I protested against those who insisted that bliss was a stage to be transcended, a state to be overcome. I indulged my ecstasy, marveled at its sweet fullness, sought its constant return. It was my secret indulgence, a personal treasure which I neither revealed nor rejected.

Now, strange to say, I seem to have a different perspective. I no longer crave ecstasy. I value the quiet moments, the lovely small happenings that ornament the day. I long for stability, well-being, good health, abundant energy for the familiar tasks. I have a new mantra: "Be steady. Be steady. Be steady."

Partly, I think, I am longing for inner balance in order to avoid the dramatic swings between pleasure and pain that I typically experience when rapture returns. Partly I am trying to deal more directly with the various aches and pains that accompany the aging process. (I don't like to admit to these—after all, Kundalini is supposed to cure all ills.)

And I am also seeking strength to look more fully at the pain and suffering in the world, some near at hand among friends, some in other parts of the world. The load of grief among sentient beings is immense, and I do not want to reject awareness of this fact.

Moreover, I have had a full cup of ecstasy in my life. My hunger has been assuaged. It is like a favorite food or distant land that one experiences or revisits until satiety is reached. One does not refuse the repetition of the experience. But one no longer "has to have it" in one's life.

Yet, having said all of this, I know that the bliss will return, in its own time and on its own terms. Again and again, I have declared the end of bliss, and always I have been proved wrong. Sometimes it is weeks or even months between recurrence. But then a piece of music, a quiet meditation with a circle of friends, a meeting with an advanced soul or loving friend—can awaken the old energies, send the self once more into the transcendent reality that (at the moment) takes precedence over all else.

This morning, I woke up with a great sense of despair over the recent events in our country. I am sure many, many others share my grief. Once more, my shoulder seemed to be out of place, and the pain in my upper back was insistent.

I dawdled through breakfast, glanced at a few daily news items (could I really bear knowing the reality of what had happened?). I thought of my childhood, which was spent in a very "conservative" small town environment (Oklahoma), and how much social progress has taken place since then (I was born in 1928—so that would be over seventy years of struggle for social equality.).We had no "Negro problem" in our town. The city fathers had long since passed a law banning the presence of African Americans after sundown. Gay marriage? Not an issue, since most people had not even heard of them (us), and if they were mentioned at all it was in whispers and disgust (after all, these were clearly "perverts," just as the psychology books of the time averred). Jews? We had never seen any, until during WWII a Jewish family bought a small clothing store on Main Street. They turned out to be hard working, solid folk who soon won the respect of the community.

Almost the only bit of diversity we had were a few Catholic families scattered in. The Baptists and the fundamentalists, of course, preached that the Catholic Church was the Great Beast of Revelations. But others among us looked on them as somehow special, in some way connected to mysteries we were not familiar with.

What are now called the religious right were then the Baptists (against smoking and dancing and certainly sex outside of marriage and other unmentionable misdeeds) plus a few Pentecostals and other fundamentalist groups.

Almost all of us (except for a few German farmers) were named Jones and Thompson and Pearce and Talbot and Smith (and Walters) and other typical Anglo-Saxon names.

The point is, the extreme fundamentalists were there and influenced many, but they were not really in control (in part because the "givens" named above were accepted with little question by almost everyone else but not much talked about). Even my Baptist classmates turned out for the senior prom, and danced with the rest.

So during my life I watched great and meaningful social progress on all these fronts—notable forward movement on issues of acceptance and diversity in my hometown and throughout society. We have come a long way, and things are not perfect, but they are indeed better all around.

And so, after yesterday, I began to wonder what was happening, if all the great improvements of the last half century were to be swept away, and we were to return to the "dark ages" of my youth. Were we entering Huxley's *Brave New World*? Orwell's *1984*? Were we watching a Greek tragedy, in which the hero would fall because of overweening pride (though he himself had never read a Greek tragedy)? Were we a nation of lemmings, rushing over the cliff to the sea?

How could we survive such a restricted world? Would women once more be driven back to their kitchens, and gays back into their closets? What would happen to the minorities and the oppressed, and people in need? Would we continue to be given slogans and clichés of reassurance, while the reality was carefully hidden from the populace at large?

I decided to do my little "practice," in part to see if I could reduce the tension locked into my body. First, as always, I bowed to the Beloved Within (was she there today? Would she come for states of pain as well as bliss?). I did a few preliminary stretches, and then began to do the first of the two *chi gong* forms I have finally managed to learn. They are simple, slow movements that follow (rather than lead) the energetic flow within. Immediately, I felt a soft tingling in my root, the source of all our "spiritual" and creative energy. It was confirmation of the abiding connection. It said, "Yes, I am here."

Then, I raised my arms level with my heart, and there it was—a soft, gentle, almost imperceptible sensation of—love, renewal, blissful sustaining presence. I caught my breath as the heart once more was subtly opened to awareness of the sacred.

So I continued my chi gong practice for another twenty minutes or so, and then I paused to commune silently with the Inner Teacher. I asked for direction in this time of need. And the answers came:

First, keep your connection with your inner guide. You guide is present always, ready to lead and help you.

Do your spiritual practice (whatever that may be) with regularity. It will keep the connection strong in adversity, and remind you who you are.

Hold your friends and special companions close. You will sustain each other in remarkable ways. You are explorers together, and wonders are unfolding.

Keep in mind that this is a time of continuing discovery and renewal as well as seeming loss and catastrophe. Think of the Taoist yin/yang symbol, which reveals how the seed of the future already exists in the present. Remember that the forces of the spirit (the large Spirit) are invisible to the eyes of those focused solely on material aims.

Review your own life. Think of the many obstacles (social, personal, and other) that you faced and overcame. Think how much joy, how much growth, how much creativity you have experienced. What a rich life you have had, a grace that was given, often a gift born of suffering.

Above all, think of your own spiritual awakening, and how it has revealed the majestic profile of something beyond ordinary human perception. You may not exist always in fully transcendent awareness, you may be dismayed at what you see taking place in the "outer" world, but you carry within the knowledge of another reality, and know what is possible despite external appearances.

Indeed, "something is happening," and we are a vital part of that transformation. We are charged with "carrying the vibration," preserving the awakening consciousness, helping humanity reach a new level of awareness.

Greet your friends in joy, band together to explore the possibilities now flooding into earth. Who knows what helpers are there? Who can say what the outcome will be?

SUDDEN GLORY, SPIRITUAL BYPASS, FINDING WISDOM

Recently, when I was describing my earlier experience of spontaneous awakening to a friend, she suggested that I had undergone "spiritual bypass." As I understand this term, it means that you leap over your chronic psychological or emotional issues to reach a sudden point of illumination or transcendence. Ultimately, you are pulled back to the mundane world where all the unresolved problems are waiting patiently for your return.

The image I have often used for this process is: at first, you are lifted on eagle's wings to the top of the mountain, where you gaze in awe at the landscape unfolding below, and the celestial beings circling above. In this state, you experience intense rapture of sprit and body. You feel, "Ah, yes, this is where I belong, where I have always lived, though I didn't know it. At last, I have come home."

Then one morning you wake up and find yourself at the bottom of the mountain. You struggle to climb up again, only this time you go on hands and knees.

Now, my question is this: have you truly undergone "spiritual bypass" in order to attain what is (seemingly) a false awakening? Is there something wrong with you because you cannot maintain your exalted state on a permanent basis? Did you fail to do your inner work prior to illumination, and hence were not really prepared for the experience?

If any one of us waited until we were perfect—intellectually, spiritually, psychologically—for the transcendent moment, none of us would ever glimpse the luminous realms, even for an instant. We would wait forever, striving, struggling, wondering if the rumors of the ultimate were true or not.

Some point to the presumed masters or gurus who apparently live in perpetual bliss states as the ideal, and dismiss our more transitory experiences as unimportant.

But the fact is—we have been to the top of the mountain. We carry within us the knowledge that bliss is attainable, that the Other is also the Within, that we may never fully comprehend our experience, but nothing can erase it from memory or invalidate its significance.

And so we, like everyone around us, continue to labor on the old issues, the familiar challenges. Nonetheless, we are transformed, and through it all we gradually find our way to the path of wisdom.

And, from time to time, we relive in momentary flashes, in sudden inner opening to rapture, the original experience. Once again, we find ourselves in bliss, and remember our true nature.

THE STAGES OF ENLIGHTENMENT

We tend to speak of "enlightenment" as if it were a single thing, a fixed level of being (consciousness). But there are in fact many stages of enlightenment, and we need to distinguish between them in our thinking. Here is one approach to the topic. The stages are not mutually exclusive, and often overlap.

The first level is that referred to in the classical literature of India and the East. It is the phenomenon of "awakening" that occurs when the yogic practitioner succeeds in bringing the energies through the chakras up to the crown, at which point divine bliss enters the head as a stream of effulgent energy and the yogi realizes that this great field or source of endless creative outpouring is the ultimate reality. She then grasps that one's own sense of self (ego) is delusion and that each of us is merely a minuscule particle in this great wave of divine pulsation that creates and maintains the cosmos.

This state of knowing can also be attained through spontaneous awakening of the Kundalini, rather than after years of dedicated practice. Near-Death Experience can also bring a similar result, in terms of the recognition it brings.

Often these states are accompanied with a profound sense of "Oneness" in a literal sense, as the initiate identifies with all that her eyes encounter, both human and other. The world may be infused with great beauty, as if the "mystery" had at last unveiled. She sees with "saint's eyes" and responds with "beginner's mind."

The second stage of Enlightenment is that of integration. The practitioner, whatever his/her background and culture, and however the awakening has occurred, must come to terms with this totally transformative experience. She must find a way to interpret what has happened in a way that is comprehensible with respect to her own world view and life story. She needs a stable foundation, a mental accompaniment for the new experience, whether this comes from traditional perspectives or authentic teachers or her own reading and investigations, or guidance from the "inner guru."

Furthermore, she will now be open to entirely new streams of energy originating from within and (seemingly) entering from outside her own body. She is literally being refashioned into a new being, and this renovation involves every cell and system in her physical body and each facet of her psyche. Her outlook and life practice will now become something quite different from her former "ego-self." She must learn to "ride the wave" of this new energetic body, to act in accord with its directions, to follow rather than try to lead or coerce it into new configurations.

The third is a level that only certain initiates will seek or achieve. It is not a requirement, but functions as an extra benefit. It has to do with seeking and incorporating a greater scope of "world knowledge" into the new scheme. The disciple will explore many fields of investigation— world history, archaeology, political systems, art and poetry, religion and philosophy, the new science, and others, and see them in a new perspective, one not inherent in most scholarly or academic approaches.

These will give added depth and texture to the original experience, which was intimately personal (as well as universal). She will thus fuse knowledge of both Eastern and Western approaches to culture and human experience, and develop the capacity to share these insights with the world at large.

The last stage is the most critical. The central lesson of the awakening was the all-pervasive reality of the giant field of love of which the cosmos is constructed, whether that field is named Brahma or god or Allah or Shiva or the goddess or the Beloved Within or the Great Father or simply "The Divine." The field itself and the energies it projects is the reality.

Now this truth is embodied in the human who is in fact enlightened, full of light, a carrier of divine love and nurturance to the world, whether in the context of daily contacts or personal service or revelation through artistic endeavor or other means. And—the human vessel of love does not even need an encompassing philosophy or schema to express the love force.

Furthermore, some attain this state in the ordinary course of their human life activities, without passage through a specific moment of awakening. The humblest among us performing the lowliest task can function as a vehicle of love. No degrees or formal ceremonies are required. As Ram Dass says in the title of his latest book, we can each "Be Love Now." We can do this in our daily lives, and thus we can so be enlightened moment by moment.

MORE THOUGHTS ON ENLIGHTENMENT

Some people try to reach enlightenment through reading and study alone. In yoga philosophy there is a branch called "jnana" yoga, suitable to these disciples. Yet though intellectual exploration of all kinds will do a great deal to build a strong foundation for later awakening, mind alone cannot take you there. At a certain point, after you have studied and considered, pondered and tested, you come up against a brick wall.

To get through the wall, you must allow the mind to dissolve completely. You must surrender all your attachments to concepts, notions, ideas. You must arrive naked at the source, and thus you must strip away all your mental armor, which now becomes a hindrance, not an aid, in your forward progress. As Bhagwan Shree Rajneesh (Osho) said, "The mind must drop before enlightenment can occur."

Let us suppose that you have never heard a bird sing but you long to do so. You will not get your wish by reading books about birds, or cataloguing all the known species of fowl. Only if you set aside your books and go out into nature and sit still and listen will you hear the music you are seeking. But of course, to do this, you must go where the birds are—and you must have ears able to hear.

But even if you do give up mental seeking for Oneness, there is no guarantee that you will find it. I believe that for this, an act of grace is required. You can only wait and pray, prepare yourself in whatever way you can for the supreme moment, which may or may not come.

Therefore, it is best to continue on your path from wherever you are—incorporating not only text but practice, allowing sweet energies to flow when they come, encouraging your own psyche to unite with the beauty about you, and, above all, feeling and giving love to others who enter your life, even from a distance. Remember compassionate action. Find ways to better the world. Seek out fellow travelers who will encourage you on your journey. Learn from teachers but never fully surrender your power to external authority. Your "inner guru" will lead you to whatever level is best suited for you at this stage of your life.

THE ONLY CONSTANT

The only constant in Kundalini is change. However you begin, whether in slow progression from stage to stage (and even then the result is not guaranteed) or in some sudden, shocking opening—your initial state won't last. Your energies may shift from faint stirrings to strong pulsations, or go the other way—from dynamic to gentle. You may have periods of extreme bliss interspersed with painful or even dry spells, when it seems that nothing much is happening to move you forward. You may think you have finally arrived at balance, only to find yourself plunged once again into tumultuous feeling.

No one knows why these dramatic shifts occur, who is most susceptible to them, what the outcome will be. We only know the variations are endless, like the undulating colors which comprise a sunset, or the endlessly changing patterns of waves striking against the shore.

Some people wish to "control" the ceaseless interplay of the energies, to tame them through harsh disciplines. Others prefer to follow the inner guide, enjoying the play within as the unseen teacher leads the way. In a real sense, this dichotomy reflects patriarchal vs. matriarchal attitudes, mechanical vs. organic approaches, controlling vs. allowing.

I am of the latter persuasion. For me, too much discipline is intrusive, an arbitrary imposition of form on an intrinsically formless experience. I look on Kundalini as ultimate gift, visitation of the divine. How then could I presume to override such majestic intelligence, which has graced me by entering my life and leading me to ever deepening mystery?

This is not a melody already scored, nor a drama previously scripted. It is an ever new, constantly fresh revelation, just as this year's blossomings are not those of the year before.

THE NEW CHILDREN

Something is happening. The children coming to us today are often quite different from those we have known before. I know because I read about them, see them as prodigy performers, and hear their stories from their parents who are my friends.

Here are a few sample stories:

One night as my friend was putting her little girl of about six to bed, her daughter announced, "God is love." When the mother asked where she had heard this, her child answered, "at school." Now, this mother was very perplexed since the school her daughter attended was not one that would include such teaching. So she asked, "What school are you talking about?" So her daughter explained that after she went to bed each night, she went to "a different school" where she learned things like this.

Another child told her mother the following "dream":

In the dream, everything had turned to dust. No people or animals were left, but god was still there, playing in the playground. Somehow, this account reminds me of the Vedic notion that the world is merely "leela," god's play.

In recent years, we have heard from many children who describe past lives with great precision and convincingness. Likewise, there are numerous stories from children of their Near-Death experiences. All of these suggest that there is a great deal more to consciousness itself than we had assumed.

However, for me the most fascinating area of children's "expanded consciousness" is presented in the recent book by Dr. Wayne Dyer and Dee Garnes called *Memories of Heaven*. This book is a collection of children's "recollections" of the time before they were born while they were, in their terms, living in "heaven." These accounts come from children two, three, or four years old, who longed to return to their paradisal state before they were born.

One narration tells of a very small boy who unexpectedly burst into tears. When his mother asked him why he was crying, he said he missed his mother. When she explained that she was his mother, he answered that he missed his other mother, the one he had had in heaven before he came to earth. This mother was total love and he yearned to be with her again.

Another small girl explained that she missed her other (heavenly) mother and also god. When she was asked what God looked like, she answered that god was a being of light and that He was filled with love.

When one little child was asked what she missed about "heaven," she explained that she felt at home there and nothing bad ever happened.

I found these accounts extremely moving. I myself have long believed that consciousness exists before birth and continues after what we call death. These descriptions "out of the mouths of babes" confirm what I have long sensed. And for me, the divine love that is central to each telling is what I have called Kundalini, the love that sustains us as we move through our human forms and that will enfold us totally when we "go home."

LIVING IN THE TWO WORLDS

Recently, I was moving slowly and listening to music when it happened. For half an hour or so I felt once more the "exquisite bliss" of the divine energies. I stroked my "aura" (mostly arms and chest) for many minutes—my head opened, chest, torso, arms, wrists, hands—everything was merely bliss waves. Again, I was surprised by this unexpected "visitation" from the unseen. It has now been over twenty years since my awakening.

At this stage, what many of us are learning is how to swing back and forth from "bliss consciousness" to ordinary, or rational, consciousness. To swoon in sensuous delight, then focus our minds on the ordinary, the familiar—to write coherently about abstract ideas, follow a movie, read the newspaper, interact with others socially, manage all the necessary activities of the quotidian. And that is the trick—now one, now the other, now exaltation, now the daily, to "live in the world and out of it."

KUNDALINI RISING
AND COLLECTIVE CONSCIOUSNESS

More and more it is happening. One day, you are going along, doing your usual things, thinking your usual thoughts, when—bam! seemingly out of nowhere, a shock wave goes through your system. You feel something happening within which is totally different from anything you have ever experienced before. Ecstatic energies seem to flood your system, perhaps opening the lower portions of your body, perhaps surging upward, enlivening and awakening areas in ways completely foreign to you before this moment.

You ask, "What is going on?" The experience continues, bringing periods of exquisite bliss as well as bizarre behaviors and sometimes pain. Sooner or later, you discover or stumble upon the answer: you have experienced Kundalini awakening.

Of course, the pattern varies from person to person. The awakening may be triggered by trauma, illness, events of dramatic intensity of all sorts. It may be brought on gradually, perhaps through traditional meditation or spiritual practices. It could occur simply from being in the presence of a highly developed spiritual leader and her (his) followers.

Whatever the cause, this event seems to be occurring with greater and greater frequency across the globe. No one is keeping statistics on this. Nobody really knows the overall pattern or ultimate purpose. What we do know is that "something is happening." No one fully understands it or can state its intended goal. But we can speculate as to where this phenomenon is headed.

The current issue of a recent periodical is dedicated to what is called collective intelligence. It contains many articles by well-known writers, who agree that collective knowledge and group expertise is notably more effective than individual effort in solving problems and achieving desired outcomes, especially in the world of practical affairs, from sports to global challenges. They suggest this reliance on group wisdom may be a manifestation of the evolution of human intelligence posited by many writers of our time.

Perhaps group consciousness extends to realms beyond the pragmatic. Perhaps what the mystic experiences in her state of exaltation—when she thinks and feels beyond her own boundaries, as if knowing the internal thoughts and perceptions of others as well as her own—is a clue to this new state. We are told by various channels and sources claiming knowledge of after-death states that in the spirit realm, each being has instant access to the feelings and mental states of all the others. Some speak of actual cells of consciousness, each unit consisting of a "soul group" of beings who participate in a common awareness and collective identity.

What if indeed this is our evolutionary purpose: to achieve a consciousness beyond the individual. To feel with, be with, know with others in a kind of shared empathy, while still retaining our own individual identity.

In the drug experience, people sometimes attain this kind of consciousness. They say they know intuitively what others are thinking, feel what they are feeling. And the state which makes this possible is one of overwhelming love—seeing with the eyes of love, feeling with the spirit of love. At that moment, everything is beautiful, all beings are oneself.

What if all of us reach this state through evolutionary development to another level of consciousness? What if Kundalini awakening is god exploding in our bodies, revealing our true identity as particles of the divine? What if we (our collective cell of kindred souls) had access to the accumulated wisdom and experience of the group, could share in the past spiritual development of all the others? What if we then functioned without the physical containers (bodies) which restrict, without need of the biological supports (food, water, air) which sustain us now? What if this new creation is infused with divine energy, the energy of love, the sustaining element which underlies and manifests as creation itself? What if we become fuller expressions of the divine?

What if the present world crisis provided the impetus for worldwide initiation—crisis bringing us to god? And what if we are here at this time to participate in and support this dramatic transition to a new level?

Is this the direction in which human evolution is headed? Does Kundalini put us more squarely on this path? Does it draw us closer to the next stage of human development? I think so.

We can never prove it through test or analysis. We cannot force it to come forth. We can merely let it happen, both experiencing and witnessing in silent wonder as the mystery unfolds.

THE DIVINE HUMAN

According to Ilya Prigogine, systems brought to a higher and higher level of stress will ultimately spring to a new, more complex, level of organization, or else disintegrate entirely.

What then are our chances for such a leap—a propulsion into a new consciousness, given the current strains within the common psyche? And what form might such a dramatic transformation take? What new creatures will emerge as "us?"

We could, theoretically, abdicate the realm of the material entirely, becoming creations composed of and dwelling solely in the realm of the energies (considerable evidence exists for the existence of non-local consciousness—as out-of-body experience, esp., clairvoyance, the shared intuitive and psychic experiences of twins, etc.). This shucking of the mortal casement would presumably relieve us (the community) of many of our current social problems—such as universal suffering, violence, hunger, greed, etc. Where there is nothing to covet, there is nothing to seize.

Tyranny is impractical in a realm where possessions do not exist and domination is not possible. We would, presumably, float about in radiant circles of light, free of threat or dangers. But how would our lives find focus? Toward what state or achievement would we strive? Is unbroken harmony the condition we truly desire?

Or—again—we might retain the familiar material veil, but with some sort of massive infusion of a new, transcendent principle or perspective into the society at large. This would be a grandiose and comprehensive conversion of our very way of perceiving (sensing, knowing, reacting to) the world around us. Perhaps it would be produced by a dramatic overhaul of the nervous system, possibly through widespread awakening of Kundalini power, all this conceivably triggered by astrological alignments sending new frequencies into the earth atmosphere. Or perhaps such "seed beings," selves already experiencing and issuing the new frequencies, are already among us, awakening by their very presence others who will in turn resonate to the new frequencies. Perhaps we ourselves are such beings, sent here to stimulate and embody the energies of universal transformation.

Indeed, evidence of widespread spiritual transformation is appearing all around. Some are discovering their inner connections with divine reality in unique ways. Distance hearing, distance seeing, extrasensory perception of all kinds, near-death experiences are widely experienced. Ecstasy is being reported across the globe, as subtle energies become more and more refined, more and more delicate in expression. We feel bliss in our bodies at sacred locations, in the presence of special works of art, when music turns our bodies into sounding boards, each note awakening pulsating sensuous delight within. We experience another's sweet energies in their presence. From poetry, from movement, from certain energy healers, we ourselves become vessels of rapture.

For most of us, such states of sensuous joy are not fixed permanently within. We must go through a long period of adjustment and integration, sometimes encountering difficult and even painful impediments to progress, as we clear various "blocks" that now demand to be attended to and cleared, whether these are emotional, psychological, or physical in nature. We now accept that we are "betrothed to the invisible" (John O'Donohue) and may make love with the "beloved within" on a daily basis. We may find new talents unleashed, as we "bring the gift back home" (Joseph Campbell). The world now takes on a new luminosity and favorite friends appear in all their beauty. We now know universal love for the universe and all it contains, and we realize that we ourselves are mere participants in the cosmic play, minute expressions of the energies issuing from an unseen source.

We are now in the transition stage, the interim between the old forms of being and the new selves coming to birth. But the new Self is arriving in unmistakable ways, to countless numbers across the globe, even in the midst of the chaos and violence that are erupting in many locations. Terror and beauty arrive together in our world.

We are indeed in a time of human evolution into a new formulation, and, as with any birth process, a certain amount of pain and difficulty is involved. We are allowed tastes and glimpses of the new condition, but we are still caught in the process of change itself.

At times it feels as though the world itself is spinning toward total annihilation. But even in the midst of such seeming universal disaster, we are infused by rapture, and progress toward our destined goal occurs.

Evolution occurs not in a state of tranquility but in times of acute stress and peril. Our crisis is upon us. The outcome remains to be seen.

OUR LIVES TRANSFIGURED

As we move ahead in our unfoldment, our energies become ever more refined, more sensitive, more subtle.

Again and again, when we meet people we mirror their interior energies within our own bodies. When we stand to chat with a stranger, we feel sweet bliss in our own chakras (often the lower two) and know in this way that what is open within their bodies is reflected now within our own. We sometimes are caught unaware, catapulted into ecstatic bliss by merely holding our hands a few inches away from our heads, or by standing in front of our bookcase, which contains many sacred texts.

Some of us hear celestial music (this in the company of others who hear it too). Some see visions of deities and others share the same visions with them. We feel ecstatic energy rising from the ground and entering our bodies at certain holy places. We sense as bliss the beautiful energies infused into certain masterworks of art by their creators. The world about appears in luminous transcendence on a simple walk by a stream or near flora or other growing things. Even the grass or the bark of trees takes on a special sheen. We sense the energy of flowers or plants as we move our eyes from one to another.

Music, yoga, simple micro movement, a poem, a whiff of essential oil, or a crystal can awaken extreme rapture.

We meet many others on a similar path and are grateful for their companionship.

We are not constantly in such states of transcendence, for we are in a time of transition to a higher level of realization. Yet more and more we experience oneness on an essential level, for we are each a part of the vast web of love encircling and empowering the world, the universe, the untellable mystery that is the ultimate real, though we may have no words to describe it.

Thus we progress toward our true state as divine beings and know that we are part of the vast transfiguration now sweeping the world—the actual evolution of our species into the next stage of our existence.

KUNDALINI AND THE EVOLUTION OF CONSCIOUSNESS

Before we reach enlightenment, we enjoy only temporary tastes and glimpses of this sublime awareness, so that we can know that it is real, but not a place where we can dwell permanently while we are on this earth.

Some ask, "Why are we not able to dwell within the blissful realm of Kundalini while on earth?"

In one sense, the answer is simple: we are living on earth, not in heaven; we are human, not angels. Humankind has asked from the earliest of times why we no longer dwell in paradise. Myths of the lost Golden Age appear in the lore of many, many cultures, from the story of Adam and Eve to the accounts of the yugas (eras) in Eastern literature (which descend from the earliest—the Golden Era—to our own time. We now live in the Kali Yuga, the time of strife and chaos.

However, for Kundalini, the question becomes a bit more specific. Why, having once tasted "paradise" on this earth is it so often snatched away, the bliss overturned as pain and forms of dis-ease ensue? Why can we not maintain this elevated state in which all was bathed in the bliss of overwhelming love and our bodies and souls seemed to exist (finally) in complete accord?

To begin with, we have to remember that when Kundalini is awakened we are—temporarily—more or less removed from this world into an inner Eden. We exist and feel in ways we have never experienced before. We are like babes enjoying the complete attention and devotion of mothers who dote on us and give us constant love and nourishment.

But then, suddenly, our Edenic world fades and we become aware of the pressures of the outside world. The mother-spirit vanishes (or diminishes) we are on our own in a disturbed, sometimes uncaring, sometimes threatening world. We realize we have to do more than sigh in rapture, that we have to earn a living, care for the needs of families and friends (who may be undergoing special challenges in their own lives), our own health may seem to falter. Old psychological issues may surface and demand to be attended to. Old injuries may begin to pain us again.

I think this first period is the honeymoon time of Kundalini. It can last for days or weeks or even years, but at some point (at least for all I know) it will take a different turn. The honeymoon is now over, and we must deal with some very pressing issues before we are ready to go forward to the next stage. What we have experienced thus far is a huge quantum leap into another level of existence. That part was easy. Now the real work begins. We must go back, deal with all unfinished business in our lives, learn new ways to cope with the world and its stressors, find new methods to maintain balance. This is the time of purification, of making ourselves ready to sustain these new energies and this new way of life in a more consistent way.

The first phase came to us through grace. Now we must prove our worthiness, make ourselves strong, mend all weaknesses, clear all faults (including the flaw of excessive self-rejection).

It is one thing to visit another planet as a temporary visitor. To take up residence as a permanent citizen is another matter. Our bodies must adjust to a new climate, our nerves to new energies, our systems to a new level of vibration.

It would, I believe, be much easier to make this transition in a protected environment. In earlier times, those undergoing such deep spiritual transformation went into monasteries, sought out caves, withdrew into the forest. But most of us are unable to do that. We must continue to exist in the midst of a disturbed and disturbing society, to be buffeted constantly by the knowledge of the disruptions going on around us, to withstand the shocks and traumas which accompany every day living.

We must learn to live in "the two worlds," the inner world of deep spiritual connection and the outer world of the external society.

And we must find ways to "bring the gift back home." Joseph Campbell, in his classic work, describes how the hero, after facing many arduous ordeals, captures the treasure (for us, new awareness, new ways of being) and returns to offer it to society as a whole, so that all may share.

And that, I think, is exactly what we are called to do in this particular era, when survival of the race is itself the key issue. We must forgo focusing exclusively on private salvation (now a luxury) in order to give of ourselves to the world, to help others in their life predicaments and to aid them as they too progress to higher levels.

This is the evolutionary process. It does not occur as a single, final leap into a new way of being. It is unpredictable, now advancing, now slowing, now going forward, now retreating. If we are the new New Race of Humans, we must remember that we are merely the advance models. I think those of us undergoing transformation at this time have come to the planet in order to make it easier for those who follow. They will, I believe, do it better. Their transition will be easier, their progress more steady.

Some call this process "the divinization of matter." Teilhard de Chardin spoke of advancement toward "Omega Point," where the human and the divine would meet. Many today are speaking about Evolution of Consciousness. All of these point to a similar phenomenon—the movement of humanity to a higher level of being. At times it seems like the forces of spiritual evolution are in a race with the forces of massive world destruction. No one knows how the contest will end.

Ours is not an easy assignment, but more and more are joining the ranks. Ours is not a simple task, but it is the most essential endeavor I can think of. And I feel that to be included in this effort is a blessing of the highest order.

OATMEAL AND TRANSFORMATION:
TWO RECENT EXPERIENCES

It is astonishing. It just keeps happening. And, even though it has occurred countless times before, one is convinced that the newest experiences are beyond all the others, taking us to yet another level.

I am speaking, of course, of the experience of ecstasy, a state I first encountered some forty years ago and which continues to visit from time to time even now, as I enter my ninth decade.

Here is the first:
This morning the surprise happened. I was at the computer when I realized I was feeling sweet energies here and there. On instinct, I lifted my arms face high and moved them in gentle micro movements back and forth. The rapture flowed, first inside my head and then flowing down my body. I have had many "bliss outs" in my life, but this was unlike any other. So soft, so gentle, so tender. Indeed, it was like light playing everywhere I moved my hands. Light infinitely subtle, inexpressibly loving, felt in and around the body. I am grateful.

And this a few days later: As so often is the case nowadays, it arrived unannounced and in surprising circumstances. I was in fact standing at the kitchen counter fixing some oatmeal for breakfast when I felt energies stirring here and there within. So I paid heed to them, perhaps moved my hands a bit, and then felt my lower chakras awakening. The sensation grew sweeter and sweeter, as I gently moved my hands here and there over the chakras, never touching my body. Indeed, I felt as though I were being infused with light, with rapture, with a frequency higher than any I had known before. I seemed to enter a new level of transcendence, as if I were experiencing yet another initiation, this into a realm previously unsuspected. I longed to stay forever, feeling the boundless love of the universe flow throughout my body.

I stopped just in time to save my oatmeal from burning, and spent the next few hours wondering what all of this meant, where it had come from, what its intention was.

Perhaps it was another step in becoming the divine human that many writers have talked about. Perhaps it is what the alchemists of ancient times were seeking through their various esoteric practices. Maybe it is movement toward Teilhard's Omega Point. Is this what is meant by "Enlightenment?" Is this the light body? I think that none of us have fully reached this high state as yet, but I feel that we are sometimes granted tastes or glimpses of what that condition might be.

I wonder if this is how we all existed before we incarnated and if this is how we will be once we return to our origin. All of us are involved in this process in our own ways and according to our own rhythms. Together we move toward species evolution, in a manner that seems to be orchestrated elsewhere.

In the meantime, we live in mystery.

How blessed we are to be part of this process!

May the Beloved hold you in her arms as we go through this transit together.

WHO I AM

(for Kundalini, the Beloved Within)

The Hindus call me
the serpent of love,
Shiva's own Shakti
by whom
the world is made.

In Africa,
I am "Num."
I bring blessings
and sweet healing.

The Hebrews think of me
as the Shekhinah,
and long for my presence.

The Christians term me
the Holy Spirit.
I struck down Paul
on his way to
Damascus.
I entered the room
of the disciples
during the Pentecost
when light blazed over their heads.

In Egypt I am the
magic elixir

poured down into our bodies
from the gods.

When the goddess
lived in Greece,
I moved among the dancers.

The shamans embrace me
as they fly to heaven.

I am the rapture
of the saints,
the suffering
of the betrayed.

I am inside you,
in every cell and pore.

I am without
in every stone
and star.

No one has seen me
or held me
in their hands.

I am all that is.

I am you.

SUGGESTED READINGS ON KUNDALINI

Many people encountering Kundalini for the first time as well as those involved in an ongoing process wonder where to begin their research into this unfamiliar topic. The following list is arranged more or less in the order of difficulty, with the most basic texts presented first.

Tara Springett—*Enlightenment Through the Path of Kundalini: A Guide to a Positive Spiritual Awakening and Overcoming Kundalini Syndrome*
This book is "written for everybody who wants to learn about the mysterious phenomenon of kundalini and use it to reach the pinnacle of human development—enlightenment. The book is equally written for those who are going through an involuntary awakening..."

This volume contains much valuable information from a therapist who has extensive experience in the field of Kundalini, although I do not agree with her assertion that Kundalini is a certain path to enlightenment (what is?) I also think it can be dangerous to try to trigger it through intent. I am with Gopi Krishna, who felt that the inner guide would bring spontaneous awakening when the student was ready. Of course, one can prepare for the time when that may happen in order to be fully receptive.

Bonnie Greenwell—*The Kundalini Guide: A Companion for the Inward Journey* (Inward Journey Guides) (Volumes 1 and 2)
Both volumes contain easily accessible information that is especially useful for the beginner on the path.

Gopi Krishna—*Enlightenment: The Evolutionary Energy in Man*
Gopi Krishna's Kundalini awakening is accepted as the classic account of how Kundalini awakens and operates within the human system. As a result of his experience, he became convinced that Kundalini was the driving force behind universal evolution of conscious. I agree with him, since Kundalini itself seems to bring about radical transformation of the nervous system, the mind, and the spirit. His view is especially persuasive given the current widespread accounts of Kundalini awakening reported across the globe. Further, Kundalini appears to be catching, as often one initiate triggers similar reactions in others close to them.

Lawrence Edwards—*Awakening Kundalini*
"With his unique expertise in modern psychology, neuroscience, meditation training, and spiritual traditions, Lawrence Edwards clarifies for readers the many dimensions of Kundalini awakening, including practices and meditations for recognizing its manifestations and preparing the body and mind to enter its expansive, empowering flow/..." A Jungian therapist, Lawrence is available for phone consults.

Dorothy Walters, Ph.D.—*Unmasking the Rose: A Record of a Kundalini Initiation*
Dorothy experienced spontaneous intense Kundalini awakening in 1981 in a setting (Kansas) where she did not know a single person who had even heard of Kundalini. This book offers an "inside view" of what it is like to undergo such awakening in a process that has continued to unfold over many, many years with only the guidance of the "guru within." It is one of the few accounts of the personal journey written in contemporary times. Many find this book useful as a guide for their own experience, even if theirs is merely spiritual transformation as such, in whatever guise. For the author, Kundalini is the manifestation of the "beloved with," a presence which brings recurrent experiences of ecstatic union with the divine essence, as well as many challenges along the way as she seeks to balance and integrate these unfamiliar energies. In recent years, she has focused on writing spiritual poetry and reflections on the journey which she publishes as a blog (http://www.KundaliniSplendor.blogspot.com) as well as printed texts. She takes inquiries at: dorothywalters72@gmail.com

El Collie—*Branded by the Spirit*
http://www.kundaliniawakeningsystems1.com/downloads/branded-by-the-spirit_by-el-collie.pdf
El Collie, now deceased, was a pioneer in the area of Kundalini studies. Her early newsletter (called Shared Transformation) brought myriad responses from those willing to share their experiences at a time when Kundalini was seldom spoken of. Her articles on Kundalini, expressed with eloquence and grace, are extremely insightful. Unfortunately, she herself experienced primarily the negative symptoms of Kundalini, and she suffered much pain as a result, with the result that she pays little attention to the blissful aspects of the process. Nonetheless, hers is one of the most fascinating discussions of the many features of the

Kundalini process. The first entries on this site are mainly her own earlier autobiography. The later segments (beginning around p. 61) focus more specifically on aspects of Kundalini.

Kundalini Rising—from **Sounds True**
Anthology from various perspectives—includes Dorothy Walters on the relation of Kundalini and the mystical journey.

Lee Sannella—*The Kundalini Experience: Psychosis or Transcendence*
Lee Sannella was one of the first to note the resemblance between psychological crisis and Kundalini awakening. Sometimes one is mistaken for the other. This book is of special relevance to all who are counseling those undergoing apparent spiritual awakening.

Evelyn Underhill—*Mysticism*
This book is a classic in the field of mystical scholarship. Though Underhill frames her study in terms of Christian belief systems, her presentation applies equally to all mystical traditions and lineages, of whatever disposition. Since Kundalini is itself one of the great mystical journeys, this book is extremely helpful for those Kundalini voyagers pursuing this path. Note: Skip the first section (too academic) and start with Part Two (more relevant).

Dorothy Walters, Ph.D..—*Some Kiss We Want: Poems Selected and New (second edition)* (poems reflecting the experience of Kundalini Awakening)

Dorothy Walters, Ph.D.—*The Kundalini Poems: Reflections of Radiance and Joy*

Videos on YouTube:

Dorothy Walters and **Andrew Harvey Interview**
Andrew Harvey interviews Dorothy Walters on her Awakening experience.

Dorothy Walters and **Andrew Harvey**
Several videos on YouTube

Batgap Interview by Rick Archer

Dorothy Walters and **Andrew Harvey** read the poems of *Some Kiss We Want: Poems Selected and New*
(from live performance at book launch)

Victor Oddo—*Kundalini Awakening : 11 Classic Signs of a Kundalini Awakening*

AFTERWORD
KUNDALINI AND THE TRANSITION

Just as this book was about to go to press, a new and unexpected danger emerged, wreaking havoc wherever it appeared. Traveling swiftly across borders and even continents, it made its presence known by casualties and deaths numbering in the many thousands. Some felt that this plague was God's punishment for a populous committed to material rather than spiritual values. Others saw the great loss of life as a necessary preparation for actual mutation of the species, as old institutions collapsed and new perspectives arose.

I myself believe that yet another factor is involved.

Some question why we might focus on a topic as "esoteric" as Kundalini with its potential for ecstasy and a sense of divine union when so many are in evident suffering and pain. I feel that the answer may be suggested by the famous yin/yang symbol, where the seed of the counter impulse is present in the center of the dominant field. A major spiritual awakening is occurring across the globe even in the midst of the outer chaos and confusion. The world is, in fact, collapsing (externally) and being reconfigured within all at the same time.

Kundalini is indeed an essential factor in this time of transition. It can indeed provide us with the impetus and energy to build a new world, for we ourselves are becoming a radically reconstructed version of the "human" species. By a mysterious process the caterpillar becomes the butterfly, just as now the seemingly ordinary person is often transforming in unexpected ways.

The early alchemists worked in secret to turn the base metal of the familiar self into the gold of the divinized human. The Kabbalists sought to ignite a process of transfiguration for the species. What Ramana Maharshi longed for and Teilard de Chardin envisioned is happening here, now, and we are a vital part of that awakening. We are like the yogis of old who sought through discipline and devotion to bring themselves into closer alliance with the divine. Our work is to be open to the new frequencies, to allow our inner and outer selves to be transformed into a new formulation of what it means to be "human." We are the "seeds" of the coming world and we are unfolding across the planet. Ours is an exciting time as one era gives way to another as yet not fully defined stage in our evolution. The transition is not always easy and the outcome is not guaranteed, but we are, I believe, blessed to be included in this process. It is why we came.

AUTHOR'S NOTE

Dorothy Walters, Ph.D., spent most of her professional life as a professor of English literature in various Midwestern universities. She helped to found one of the early women's studies programs in this country and served as the director of this program for many years. After an extended residence in San Francisco, Dorothy now lives and writes in Colorado, where she has a close relationship with the mountains as well as various streams and canyons.

Dorothy underwent major Kundalini awakening in 1981 (a phenomenon totally unfamiliar to her as well as to most of her contemporaries at the time); since then she has devoted her life to researching and writing about this subject and to witnessing the unfolding of this process within herself as well as assisting others on a similar path through writing and other means. As someone who made her extensive journey without the direction of any external leader or guru, church, or established lineage, she is a strong believer in the "guru within," the inner guide rather than the external authority figure or institution. The reflections in this volume grow directly from that ongoing experience and reveal her inner discoveries as she went through this intense transformation.

She feels that universal Kundalini awakening is the means for planetary and personal evolution of consciousness, and that evidence of planetary initiation is becoming more and more prevalent. Both Dorothy's poetry and prose give expression to the intense experiences of both the ecstasy and pain that Kundalini may bring as we undergo this inner transformation.

Her Kundalini awakening and subsequent process of unfolding are described in her memoir, *Unmasking the Rose, A Record of a Kundalini Initiation*. Her article on "Kundalini and the Mystic Path" is included in *Kundalini Rising*, an anthology from Sounds True Publications. Her poems, which have been included in many anthologies and journals, have been set to music and sung at the Royal Opera House (in workshop spaces) in London as well as Harvard University, Boulder's Resonance Chorus, and various choirs, used as texts for sermons and read aloud in churches, included in doctoral theses, been frequently quoted, and have given inspiration to many. Recently, a pilgrim to Petra read one of her poems aloud while there. Her newest book is a collection of poems called Some Kiss We Want: Poems Selected and New. These verses give expression to the experience of Awakening into Kundalini, as it unites us with the Beloved Within.

Now in her ninth decade, Dorothy often gives counsel and referral free of charge to those undergoing spontaneous Kundalini awakening and/or spiritual transformation.

You can see a recent YouTube video of her at: Dorothy Walters and Andrew Harvey read from her "Some Kiss We Want: Poems Selected and New."

Other YouTube presentations:
"Dorothy Walters and Andrew Harvey: Interview." (Dorothy's story)
"Dorothy Walters and Andrew Harvey: Kundalini" (a conversation on this topic)
"Dorothy Walters and Andrew Harvey Read from New Works" (Andrew reads poems from "Turn Me to Gold"—translations from Kabir; Dorothy reads from "The Kundalini Poems.")

She produces a blog at http://www.kundalinisplendor.blogspot.com (Poems and Reflections on the Spiritual Journey). She can be found on Facebook at Dorothy Walters, and links to many of her works can be located at www.dorothywalters.com.

Dorothy Walters can be contacted by email at: dorothywalters72@gmail.com.

Printed in Great Britain
by Amazon